Private Capitol Punishment

The Florida Model

By

Ken Kopczynski

ISBN: 1-4184-1568-5 (e-book)
ISBN: 1-4184-1567-7 (Paperback)

Library of Congress Control Number: 2004091651

This book is printed on acid free paper.

Printed in the United States of America
Bloomington, IN

Disclaimer

All the characters and events in this book are true. The author accepts sole responsibility for the accuracy of any and all representations within its pages.

Acknowledgments

This book and the incidents reported in it could not have happened without the support of a number of individuals and organizations. At the top of the list is David Murrell, Florida PBA Executive Director. His support and guidance have been immeasurable. I first met Judy Greene, an independent criminal justice analyst, in late 1997. Judy knows the for-profit private prison industry like the back of her hand. Dave and Gaye Bachman were always there to answer my technical questions. Keith Powell deserves credit for putting up with me so long. A great big thank you goes to all the dedicated public employees at the Florida Commission on Ethics, the Florida Corrections Commission and the Office of Program Policy Analysis and Governmental Accountability. Also, thanks to Marcia Eggers for proofreading and Bob Peterson for editing and layout.

This book is dedicated to all the good folks,
fighting the good fight.

Table of Contents

Preface

In the early 1990's if you asked me what I thought about for-profit private prisons I'd have said, "Private prisons? You have to be kidding? Are there private prisons?" Ask anyone who is not a criminal justice researcher, prison activist or correctional officer the same question today and he or she will probably respond the same way. Private prisons are below the radar and the industry wants to keep it that way.

Private prisons and their corollary industries, private inmate transportation, private inmate food services and private inmate medical services, have been around since the 1980's. They are a throwback to the convict lease system that developed after the Civil War.

So what's the big deal? Who cares whether the government or a private corporation runs a prison or a jail? If a private company can run a correctional facility as well as government and for less money, then why not let them?

Private Capitol Punishment is the story of my experience into the "black hole" of prison privatization. I call it a black hole because I was pulled into the issue and have not been able to get out. I am a legislative assistant and lobbyist for the Florida Police Benevolent Association, the largest law enforcement collective bargaining agent in Florida.

It was in this capacity that I started investigating the for-profit private prison industry in Florida. Little did I know that my research and tenacity would lead to the largest civil penalty at that time by the Florida Commission on Ethics, the discrediting of the academic "guru" and Wall Street darling of prison privatization, the resignation of the executive director of the state agency that oversees the private prisons, and my thrust into the position as a leader in the fight against the private prison industry.

This is a true story of corruption, politics and for-profit private prisons. And it's not just about Florida. There are private prisons across the United States and the world.

Citizens need to be concerned about how the private prison industry uses overcrowding and budget shortfalls to "sell" their services, particularly with the prison population in the United States hovering at two million.

Citizens should be outraged that some of the same lawmakers who have drafted and passed the draconian legislation locking up more and more people, thereby creating "clients" for the industry, are members of the American Legislative Exchange Council (ALEC). ALEC is a think tank that receives funding from the for-profit private industry. Industry members have even sat on ALEC's criminal justice committee.

It is important for public officials who might be considering the "Florida Model" for overseeing private prisons to read this book. Having an agency outside the department of corrections DOES NOT WORK.

If I do my job right this book should make you mad. It made me mad when I experienced it. Profiting from the incarceration of human beings is immoral. The Catholic Bishops of the South said it the best:

> To deprive other persons of their freedom, to restrict them from contact with other human beings, to use force against them up to and including deadly force, are the most serious of acts. To delegate such acts to institutions whose success depends on the amount of profit they generate is to invite abuse and abdicate our responsibility to care for our sisters and brothers.
>
> ("Wardens from Wall Street: Prison Privatization," Catholic Bishops of the South, April 2003)

— Ken Kopczynski

The Event Horizon

My journey into the event horizon (the point at which nothing including light can escape from a black hole) of what I call the "black hole" of prison privatization began on January 8, 1997.

As a lobbyist for the Florida Police Benevolent Association (PBA) tracking criminal justice legislation I was in attendance at the Florida House Corrections Committee meeting that day. Before the regular legislative session begins in Florida, the legislature holds interim committee meetings to hash over issues, bills and agencies.

At this particular meeting the executive director for the Correctional Privatization Commission (CPC), the state agency that oversees the for-profit private prison industry in Florida, was doing a "dog and pony show" to justify the CPC's existence before the committee. The discussion that follows caught my attention and started me down a path that would lead to the largest civil penalty at that time by the Florida Commission on Ethics, the discrediting of the academic "guru" and Wall Street darling of prison privatization, the resignation of the executive director of the state agency that oversees the private prisons, and my thrust into the position as a leader in the fight against the industry:

Mark Hodges (CPC Executive Director): "…Also in the audience today, we have Dr. Charles Thomas. There may be some questions come up that we would ask him to, to answer, because he's not only studied Florida, but the United States and the World, and can answer this from a national perspective. So we have him in the audience if you have any specific questions for him as well…"

Representative Allen Trovillion (Chair): "Yes, ah, Dr. Thomas…Where is Dr. Thomas? There he is. Would you have anything that you'd like to say, ah, quickly? Or I understand that, ah, you're an FSU professor. Naw,

I was just kidding (laughter). We…we're, we're all Gators (University of Florida mascot). I heard where you're from.

Dr. Thomas: "I'd be happy to answer any questions but…"

Trovillion: "Does anyone…"

Thomas: "…I don't have anything specific today."

Trovillion: "Dr. Thomas is a professor at the University of Florida and has been working now on this for some time."[1]

At the end of the meeting I asked a lobbyist for the Florida Department of Corrections (DOC) who Dr. Thomas was. She said he was the director of the Private Corrections Project at the University of Florida doing research on prison privatization and he consulted for the CPC.

The Private Corrections Project was formed in 1989 but dates back to 1982 when Thomas and an associate received a grant from the state to conduct a cost-benefit analysis of a privately managed residential program for juvenile offenders.[2]

The red flags went up. I wondered: "Who funds Dr. Thomas' Project?"

So I called Dr. Thomas at the University and asked him, "Where do you get the money for your project?" He told me "Unrestricted grants and donations." After pausing as I waited for the rest of the information, I asked "From who?" Thomas told me they prefer to remain anonymous and that I'd have to call the University of Florida Research Foundation (UFRF) because they were the ones who got the money. He told me he wasn't going to give me "the bullet that I was going to shoot him with." This lack of openness piqued my interest. What was he hiding?

Dr. Thomas continued that he'd be happy to send me copies of his work on privatization if I wanted. I told him I'd love to have copies, which he did send to me.

I called the UFRF and talked with Pearl Bigfeather, Executive Assistant for Financial Affairs. I asked her the same question I posed to Thomas: "Where does Dr. Thomas get his money for the Private Corrections Project?" She told me the same thing Thomas said: "Unrestricted grants and donations" but she continued that the Foundation was a direct support organization and not subjected to the "Government in the Sunshine

Laws." If I wanted contributor names, Ms. Bigfeather continued, I would have to get Dr. Thomas to authorize their release.[3]

In early March 1997, my source with the DOC, gave me a copy of a memo from the University of Florida Provost Office.[4] This memo provided a listing of $78,000 in private sponsor funding for the Private Corrections Project for Fiscal Year 1995 – 1996.[5] It disclosed that for-profit private prison vendors, such as Corrections Corporation of America, Wackenhut Corrections Corporation and Cornell Corrections, were underwriting Dr. Thomas' research to the tune of seventy thousand dollars.[6]

I called Sheri Austin, who was listed on the memo, at the Provost's Office and asked her for any and all information related to the funding of the Private Corrections Project for the past five years.

I also started sending out public records requests. The first went to Dr. Ron Akers, the Program Director of Criminology and Law at the University of Florida where Thomas' project resided and Mark Hodges, the Executive Director of the CPC.[7] I wanted to see what they knew about Dr. Thomas' activities.

I hit pay dirt in the Provost's Office. Sheri Austin sent me a packet with budget data for Dr. Thomas' research project over an eight-year period.[8] Thomas had collected over $270,000 from the for-profit private prison industry.[9] This was the guy who was keeping track of the industry for the CPC and determining if they were saving the state money? Talk about the fox watching the hen house!

I sent a letter to Mark Hodges at the CPC expressing the PBA's concern about possible ethics violations by Thomas.[10] I informed Hodges that Thomas had taken in large amounts of money from the industry for his project and that "…unless actions are taken immediately to correct this appearance of a conflict of interest, including but not limited to removal of Dr. Thomas as a consultant for the CPC…we will be forced to file a formal complaint with the Ethics Commission."[11]

Hodges responded that he was gathering the information on Dr. Thomas' employment with the Commission:

3

The Commission was aware of the corporate contributions to the University of Florida. The Commission was satisfied that hiring Dr. Thomas would not violate any provisions of law. Further, I made a policy decision that Dr. Thomas would not be involved in the evaluation of proposal submittals nor in policymaking decisions.[12]

Later, John Washington, CPC Assistant Executive Director, wrote to me that the Commission was still in the process of reviewing Dr. Thomas' relationships with the industry.[13] He included a letter from Dr. Thomas to the CPC and a memo from Thomas to the University of Florida regarding my requests for information. These documents were my first glimpse at Dr. Thomas' personality. Thomas wrote to Washington:

Please be advised that I would not take lightly any allegations or claims by any person or organization that I had engaged in any form of unlawful conduct, most particularly any conduct related to my professional activities. Thus it is possible that I or my attorney will wish to interview you and others known to you to have been contacted by the FPBA for the purpose of determining whether any verbal or written statements made by any person for whom the FBPA (sic) is responsible are such that, for example, they may tend to damage my professional reputation or interfere with present or prospective business relationships.[14]

Thomas was threatening to sue the PBA and me for defamation and tortuous interference.

In Thomas' memo to Ms. Barbara Wingo, UF Deputy General Counsel, he repeats his threat to sue the PBA and me, and continues:

I regret, of course, the formal tone of this memorandum. Unfortunately, the University, acting through the Office of the Provost, already has caused to be disclosed information of a type that Chapter

240, Florida Statutes, appears to prohibit being disclosed. There is reason to believe that this information has been made available to the FPBA. There is thus cause to believe that the University has not acted in the manner that I believe would best protect the important relationships which exists between the University and the persons and corporations who have made nearly $400,000 in unrestricted gifts to the University since 1989. I urge you to act to protect that relationship to the degree provided for by law.[15]

Not only was Thomas threatening the University, he admitted taking "nearly $400,000" from the industry over the last eight years!

The next day I drafted a memo for David Murrell, the PBA's Executive Director, and Hal Johnson, the PBA's General Counsel, on what strategy I should take on the Thomas question.[16] I wrote that not only had Thomas taken in hundreds-of-thousands of dollars from the industry but his summer salary at UF was paid for by the Private Corrections Project and that the week before, Dr. Thomas was added to the Board of Directors of the Corrections Corporation of America Realty Trust, collecting $12,000 per year with an option to purchase 5,000 shares in the Trust.[17] I continued that Thomas had been and continued to collect money directly and indirectly from the for-profit private prison industry in violation of Florida Statutes. My final question was "…where do we go from here?"[18]

At this time I picked up an unusual supporter but didn't know it. In a letter to Joel Freedman, Chair of the CPC, George Zoley, CEO for Wackenhut Corrections, wrote about their "concerns regarding Charles Thomas's consulting role on behalf of the Commission."[19]

Zoley laid out four points against Thomas.[20] First, at an industry conference, Thomas revealed that he held stock in various correctional companies.[21] Thomas "lamented at length how his stock portfolio was depressed and saw no reason for it."[22] I didn't find out Thomas owned private prison stock until later.

Second, Thomas was named to the CCA Prison Realty Trust. Zoley wrote, "CCA is Wackenhut's largest competitor. It is most disturbing that Mr. Thomas would participate in their Prison Realty Trust."[23] I guess Wackenhut was okay with Thomas' lack of ethics as long as it benefited all the vendors.

Third, Zoley wrote that they believed Thomas may have received other forms of financial remuneration for special services performed outside his UF activities.[24] What did Wackenhut know but wasn't telling?

And last, he wrote:

> Our company's lobbyist has told me about a conversation with Mr. Thomas which occurred prior to the last Commission meeting at which time Mr. Thomas stated "George Zoley ought to know that I speak with market analysts three or four times a week, and if he is going to take money out of my pocket, I'm going to take money out of his pocket."[25]

Zoley summarized Wackenhut's concerns with Thomas rather succinctly: "We believe that prudent public policy would, at a minimum, require that the Commission carefully consider the appearance of impropriety which may result from the employment of advisors who have a financial stake in the outcome of any process with which they are involved."[26] I couldn't have said it better.

So began my trip into the black hole of prison privatization.

The First Ethics Complaint

When Thomas took his position on CCA's real estate investment trust board, Prison Realty Trust, the *Wall Street Journal* did an expose' about his influence on the stock market.[1] The piece starts with the following question: "Is the nation's leading expert on prison privatization getting too close to his research subjects?"[2] At this time I did not know what a big fish Thomas was but I was beginning to find out.

The article continued:

> Thomas is widely considered the preeminent—as well as an impartial—guru on the fast-growing industry. He is a favorite source of reporters, too, his name appearing in at least 175 newspaper and magazine articles...Mr. Thomas' expertise has made him well-known on Wall Street, too. Statistics he publishes in his annual study of prison privatization, known as the "Blue Book," routinely appear in the research reports of securities analysts.[3]

No wonder Thomas could seriously threaten to take money out of Wackenhut's pocket! (See Event Horizon) He had the ear of Wall Street analysts.

But some were starting to express caution.

An independent analyst is quoted in the *Wall Street Journal*, "Prudent prospective investors should consider discounting any positions which rely on (Mr. Thomas's) research."[4]

Thomas' ship had started to take on water.

At the May 29, 1997 Correctional Privatization Commission (CPC) meeting, the issue of Dr. Thomas and his position on Prison Realty Trust's board was on the agenda.[5] Thomas characterized the controversy as a "perception problem" stemming from the Florida PBA requests and a complaint from Wackenhut. Thomas said the PBA's concerns

7

were politically driven by the privatization of corrections while Wackenhut's were the result of competition with CCA.[6]

At this meeting Thomas revealed publicly that he owned stock in the industry. I about hit the ceiling. How could he be the unbiased academic "guru" of prison privatization at the same time he had a direct financial interest in the success or failure of the industry? Thomas explained:

> That has been a matter of record. It's been widely covered in such obscure media years ago as the *New York Times* and the *Wall Street Journal*. That's hardly either new or secret information that is in violation of no policy, rule or procedure of the State University System or a Statute or as to applicability to the Privatization Commission. However, because there is research funding provided through gifts and donations from the University and because I do own, not huge amounts but, I do own stock in some of the private corrections management companies, the one thing that I have never done in Florida or in any other jurisdiction and I do a lot of consulting work with other Governmental entities, I do not ever as a consequence of those two things, ever participate in the evaluation of any proposal that is submitted to any other governmental agency whether to you or any other unit of government.[7]

Later, an enterprising reporter for the *Gainesville Sun*, the University of Florida's hometown paper, got Thomas to admit to owning 30,000 shares of CCA stock worth $600,000 at that time.[8]

At this same CPC meeting, Commissioners voted to approach the Ethics Commission on their own to try and get an advisory opinion before I formally filed a complaint.[9] The Commission was desperate to continue using Dr. Thomas but the pressure from the PBA and Wackenhut had become too much.[10]

Hodges wrote to the Ethics Commission about the discussion on Thomas at the Correctional Privatization Commission meeting.[11] He wrote that the Commission used Thomas since its inception in 1993 and that Thomas "is generally recognized as the nation's leading expert on the economic, legal, and policy implications of correctional privatization."[12]

In an attempt to soften the ethical conflict between Thomas and the industry via his Private Corrections Project at the University of Florida, Hodges says that because of the "unrestricted donations made by private corrections management firms" Thomas was not involved in the evaluation of proposals submitted to the Commission.[13]

Hodges asked the Ethics Commission the following:

(1) Given the limited nature of Dr. Thomas' relationship with the Commission, considering the steps the Commission has taken to avoid relying on Dr. Thomas in a manner that might give rise to a conflict of interest, does the Commission's present practice in the employment of Dr. Thomas give rise to a prohibited conflict of interest?

(1)(a) If and only if the answer to the initial question is in the affirmative, what are the additional and reasonable means by which the Commission could so structure its relationship with Dr. Thomas in such a way that the conflict of interest would be neutralized?

(2) Given the limited nature of Dr. Thomas' relationship with the Commission, considering the steps the Commission has taken to avoid relying on Dr. Thomas in a manner that might give rise to a conflict of interest, and presupposing that the proposed initial public stock offering of the CCA Prison Realty Trust is successful, would the persistence of the existing relationship between the Commission and Dr. Thomas be improper on the ground that reliance on Dr. Thomas by the Commission would give rise to a conflict of interest?

(2)(a) If and only if the answer to question number two is in the affirmative, what was the additional and reasonable means by which the Commission could so structure its relationship with Dr. Thomas in such a way the conflict of interest would be neutralized?[14]

Mark Hodges was so desperate to continue using the services of Thomas that he deflected criticism of Thomas onto the Correctional Privatization Commission. Hodges wrote to the Ethics Commission "it is our judgment that we are raising a question regarding the conduct of the Commission rather than the conduct of Dr. Thomas."[15] If Hodges only knew that the CPC would soon be under investigation also.

I drafted an ethics complaint against Thomas after the lack of response from the Correctional Privatization Commission to my concerns about Dr. Thomas. The 30-page complaint alleged that Dr. Charles W. Thomas had a "direct and indirect interest in (private corrections) companies he is required to evaluate and regulate."[16]

My complaint raised six points against Thomas: the Private Corrections Project at the University of Florida was totally underwritten by the for-profit private prison industry; Thomas was a $50 per hour employee for the Correctional Privatization Commission; Thomas consults for financial firms with a direct interest in the industry; Dr. Thomas admitted to owning stock in the industry and speaks with market analysts regularly; he was now on the CCA Realty Trust board; and Thomas' relationship with the private prison industry was being investigated by the University of Florida (more on this later).[17]

I wrote that Thomas might be in violation of Florida ethics laws:

No public officer or employee of an agency shall have or hold any employment or contractual relationship with any business entity or any agency which is subject to the regulation of, or is doing business with, an agency of which he or she is an officer or employee...nor shall an officer or employee of an agency have or hold any employment or contractual relationship that will create a continuing or frequently recurring conflict between his or her private interests and the performance of his or her public duties...[18]

And:

(N)o officer or employee of a state agency...shall have any interest, financial or otherwise, direct or indirect; engage in any business transaction or professional activity; or incur any obligation of any nature which is in substantial conflict with the proper discharge of his or her duties in the public interest.[19]

I sent out a press release and overnighted a copy of the complaint to Dr. Thomas. Thomas faxed me a memo the next day thanking me for the "professional courtesy" of forwarding a copy of the complaint to him.[20] He then attacks the ethics complaint and me.

He wrote, "I must say that I am impressed by the sheer volume of information you were able to obtain. Would I had a similar record of success in persuading University of Florida administrators to respond to my requests! I would have been more impressed had the information been relevant to the complaint."[21]

Thomas continued, using phrases like "material misstatement of fact," "the errors of your apparent conclusions," and:

I can only assume that either you have verified with the Florida Commission on Ethics that the issue did not become moot with the end of my relationship with the Correctional Privatization Commission or the limited purpose of the complaint was a bit of political theater whose effectiveness will be judged by media reactions to your press release of June 30.

In any event, a chess match with a motivated opponent is always an interesting diversion from more serious business...[22]

Thomas wrongly believed that because his contract with Correctional Privatization Commission had ended on June 30th his prior activities did not matter. Ethics violations have a five-year statute of limitations.[23] But that didn't matter anyway because later on in the year the CPC would rehire him.

Little did I know that I had now passed through the event horizon and into the black hole of prison privatization, forever changing my life.

The Convict Lease System and The Murder of Martin Tabert

In 1921, Martin Tabert, a twenty-one year-old native of North Dakota, ventured out from the family farm to see the world.[1] He had worked the farm while his brothers fought in World War I. Tabert planned to work part-time while moving from place to place. His plans came to an end in a Tallahassee, Florida rail station.

Tabert ran out of money and made the mistake of riding the train without a ticket. He was caught on December 15, 1921 by a Leon County deputy sheriff and charged with "stealing a ride on a railroad train." After being found guilty and fined $25 Tabert was turned over to the Putnam Lumber Company, which had a contract with Leon County to lease county convicts to labor at its camps—"convict leasing."[2]

The convict lease system had developed in the South after the Civil War as an attempt to recoup the labor from freed slaves and the rising costs of jails and prison.[3] The state or county "leased" inmates to logging, mining or turpentine interests who in-turn had to feed, clothe, house and care for those inmates.[4] This led to abuses such as what happened to Tabert.

The Leon County Commission was given $20 per month per inmate from Putman Lumber so the Sheriff had a financial interest in arresting money-less men for vagrancy.[5] Martin sent a telegram requesting money from his family.[6] The Tabert family sent $75 to the Leon County Sheriff only to have the money returned "unclaimed."[7] Martin Tabert had already been sent to the labor camp.

The Tabert family did not hear a word about their son until they received a letter from the Putnam Lumber Company in February the next year.[8] The letter informed the Tabert family that Martin Tabert had died in their camp on February 1, 1922 of "fever and complications" and was buried in a cemetery near the camp.[9]

Not satisfied with the explanation provided by the Lumber Company into Martin's death, the Taberts started an investigation.[10] This investigation determined how Martin had fallen into the hands of the Lumber Company via the convict lease system, something very foreign to the North Dakota family. Later developments showed they were also lied to.[11]

The first indication that something was wrong with the explanation by Leon County and Lumber Company officials given to the Tabert family came in July 1922. An ex-convict named Glen Thompson contacted the Tabert family inquiring if they wanted to know the truth behind Martin's death.[12]

What Thompson related was an exposé into the convict lease system's brutal treatment and torture of inmates. Thompson detailed Martin Tabert's death:

> In the last week of January…Martin was turned up by Cap. Willis for a whipping who reported that Martin was slow in his work and complained of being sick, but that he himself did not think so. The whipping boss was in no mood to use the strap so he postponed it for two nights. On Friday night he called Martin out of line and by a bonfire and before about 85 convicts he whipped Martin about 35 to 50 licks with a 4 inch strap five feet long, 3 ply leather at the handle, 2 ply half way down and I am told the strap weighs $7^1/_2$ pounds….The state law of Florida says that there shall be but 10 licks with the strap for each offense.
>
> Martin begged to be let loose, but his speech was not distinct and it seemed he was so weak he could not talk plain. The whipping boss put his feet on Martin's neck to keep him from moving out of position as he whipped him. When he let Martin up, Martin started back to get a bottle of medicine that had dropped out of his pocket, or had been taken out, and the whipping boss drove him into line with the big strap hitting him over the head, shoulders and back.
>
> On Saturday the next day I helped Martin get off a flat car as he came from work to camp. On Sunday morning he was sick and blind with fever….

Martin, on this Sunday morning that I speak of, was allowed to be taken in to his bunk and seemed unconscious. From that time on he could not give us his own name or where he was from…

Martin up to the time of his death only called for water, saying wa-ter. The Dr. came, I think, on Monday and left some medicine and emphasized giving quinine. On Wednesday he came. Looked Martin over and said he would not live until morning. He died a few minutes after 8:00 o'clock without a struggle…[13]

As more convicts came forward with their testimony about Martin's death the Tabert family grew furious. They asked the North Dakota State Attorney to go to Florida and investigate their son's brutal murder for nothing more than "riding on a train without a ticket."[14]

North Dakota State Attorney G. Grimson substantiated every detail in statements made in letters received by the Taberts, leading to the formation of a committee and a resolution by the Cavalier County Commission in North Dakota condemning Martin Tabert's death and calling for an "effort to bring the offenders of law to trial."[15]

The "Martin Tabert Committee" requested the North Dakota legislature to pass a resolution presenting the facts of Martin's death to the Florida Legislature. The resolution charged that Tabert died as a result of "physical abuse and torture inflicted upon him by a Putnam Lumber Company employee" and accused "Sheriff Jones and the Putnam Lumber Company of conspiring to mislead Tabert's parents concerning their son's death."[16]

Instead of sharing "the same sense of indignation felt by the people in Tabert's home state," some Florida officials lashed back at the North Dakota resolution.[17] Florida Governor Hardee claimed, "No state treated convicts more humanely than Florida."[18]

The Florida Legislature though, took the North Dakota resolution very seriously and formed a joint committee to investigate not only Tabert's death but to investigate any convict camp "wherein it has been publicly charged by the press or otherwise cruelty to convicts has occurred."[19]

At the same time a grand jury was seated in Madison, Florida to determine the guilt of Walter Higginbotham, the whipping boss, into the murder of Martin Tabert.[20] On April 12, 1923 the grand jury indicted Higginbotham and demanded a trail for the murder of Tabert.[21]

The legislative investigation committee also started taking testimony into Sheriff Jones and determined via his own testimony that he netted about $15 after expenses for every convict sent to the lumber camp.[22] The Committee concluded that Sheriff J. R. Jones and County Judge B.F. Willis should be removed from office.[23] One particular witness, Jerry Poppell, an ex-jailer, testified:

> Poppell [the ex-jailer] testified that Jones used two automobiles, bringing them back full of prisoners each night.
>
> "We would get back to the court house," testified Poppell, "late at night; and on our way in Sheriff Jones and we deputies would tell the prisoners the best thing for them to do would be to enter a plea of guilty. On our arrival at the court house, sometimes as late as 10 o'clock at night, all of them who where willing to plead guilty were arraigned."
>
> "How would you get the county judge there at that time of night?" Senator John P. Stokes asked the witness.
>
> "Oh," responded the witness, "he would be sitting here all the time with his demijohn."
>
> "His what?" Senator Stokes queried.
>
> "His demijohn with which he used to get drunk!" Poppell replied.
>
> "Did you ever get drunk yourself?" he was asked.
>
> "Yes, t'aint no use lying about it." He replied.
>
> "Then the sheriff was drunk, the deputies were drunk, you were drunk and the county judge was drunk?" asked Senator Stokes.
>
> "Yes sir."

"And you would gather there, all of you drunk, and try people for being drunk?"

"Yes sir."[24]

In the seven months prior to his receiving a commission, Sheriff Jones delivered only twenty men arrested riding the trains without a ticket to the Putnam Lumber Company — in the seven months after getting a commission Jones arrested 154 men, netting the Sheriff about $3,750.[25] Because of the reprehensible actions of Sheriff Jones and Judge Willis, they were both removed from office.[26]

Dr. T. Caper Jones, the doctor who examined Martin Tabert and pronounced him dead of "pneumonia with malaria complications," was referred to the State Board of Medical Examiners and officially denounced by the Senate as a "disgrace to the profession."[27]

The Committee charged C.H. Kennerly with the task of locating Martin's grave, having the body exhumed and given a decent burial or returned to his parents in North Dakota.[28] Kennerly encountered a hostile crowd upon arrival in Clara to find Tabert's body and could not follow through with his task.[29] Martin Tabert is still buried somewhere in the swamps of Dixie County, Florida.

The trial against Walter Higginbotham began on May 17, 1923 in Cross City but had to be moved to Lake City in Columbia County because the state felt it could not find a "qualified jury" and that an "impartial trial" could not be held in Dixie County.[30] On July 7, 1923 the jury found Higginbotham guilty of murder in the second degree but his attorney appealed the change of venue.[31] The Florida Supreme Court reversed judgment and ordered a new trail.[32] The retrial never happened.[33]

The Tabert family sued the Putnam Lumber Company civilly and on November 29, 1923 they settled for the sum of $20,000, absolving the company of "all willful blame."[34]

The joint legislative investigation committee looked into other inmate abuse cases involving the convict lease system but nothing like the Martin Tabert case.[35] The Committee concluded its work on May 10, 1923 with the following recommendations: "the county convict-lease system should be abolished; corporal punishment of state and

Ken Kopczynski

county convicts should be forever prohibited; and laws governing the care and housing of convicts be revised."[36]

Governor Hardee signed the "Convict Anti-Whipping Bill" bill on May 24, 1923 and the bill ending the convict lease system on May 25.[37]

The Rise of Private Prisons in Florida

After the death of Martin Tabert, the for-profit private prison industry in Florida remained dormant until the mid 1980s.

At this time, three federal agencies, the Federal Bureau of Prisons, the Immigration and Naturalization Service, and the U.S. Marshals Service, began contracting with for-profit private prison companies for detention of federal prisoners.[1]

In 1985, the Florida Legislature passed a law allowing the privatization of correctional facility operations and maintenance at both state and county facilities.[2] Corrections Corporation of America (CCA) took over management of the Bay County Jail in 1986 and the Hernando County Jail in 1988.[3] In 1989, the legislature authorized the state to contract with private firms for the construction and operation of state prisons.[4]

The Legislature created the Correctional Privatization Commission in 1993 because of problems with the Florida Department of Corrections' initial attempts to privatize prisons.[5] It should be noted that Dr. Thomas was instrumental in writing the law creating the Commission as testified to by CCA's lobbyist:

> "Don't forget (Thomas) wrote the law that we all are living under. I didn't write it, he didn't write it, no one in this room wrote it, he wrote it. He's the guy that understood enough to bring this privatization, after eight years of others trying, he understood how to get it going."[6]

The Commission was set up administratively in the Department of Management Services (DMS) — not the Department of Corrections (Florida is the only state with two departments of corrections—the "Florida Model").[7] The lobbyist for the DMS at that time was Brenda Smith, whose husband, Damon Smith, happened to be the lobbyist for Wackenhut Corrections, one of the largest for-profit private prison corporations.[8] Governor

Chiles appointed Bill Linder, the Secretary of DMS and Brenda's boss, as the Commission's first chairman.

The Correctional Privatization Commission began meeting in late summer 1993 and hired C. Mark Hodges as Executive Director in October 1993.[9] Mark had been a contract monitor for the Texas Department of Criminal Justice at Wackenhut's Kyle New Vision Facility.[10]

Hodges and the Commission immediately sent out a Request for Proposal for two 750 bed, medium custody, facilities for adult males.[11] In 1994, one contract was awarded to CCA and the other to Wackenhut. CCA's Bay Correctional Facility opened in August 1995 and Wackenhut's Moore Haven Correctional Facility opened in July 1995.[12]

From the start, it appeared the iron triangle that developed between legislators and staff, the Correctional Privatization Commission, and the lobbyists for the industry was ripe for corruption.

The funding mechanism used for the facilities built for the CPC was a Certificate of Participation (COP). COPs allow the state to avoid the required public vote for bond debt and also keep this obligation off the budget. The state or contracting agency is not liable for payments on the bond. Rather, the vendors create a finance corporation that then goes to the bond market to obtain funding for the prison construction. The bonds are backed by "rents" paid to it by the contracting agency to the finance corporation. These rents cover the vendors' construction and operating costs, and the payment of the debt service.

Because of the higher risk with a COP, these bonds carry a higher interest rate than if the state or local agency floated the bond itself because of its rating as a governmental body. This higher interest rate actually increases the cost of the facility over the usual twenty-year term of the bonds than if the governmental agency had sold the bonds itself.

Two state legislators who voted to create these first two prisons had an indirect financial interest in the selling of the bonds for these prisons.[13] Senator Daryl Jones (a Democrat from Miami) worked for the investment-banking firm of Douglas James Securities, which received $37,000 in commissions for the sale of notes on Wackenhut's Moore Haven Facility.[14]

There was $31,000 in legal fees for Senate President Jim Scott's (a Fort Lauderdale Republican) law firm for underwriting advisement for the facility.[15] Both Jones and Scott denied they had any contact with Wackenhut officials or officials overseeing the contract.[16]

After contracting for two more adult facilities, and four juvenile facilities that were eventually transferred to the Department of Juvenile Justice (except for CCA's Lake City Facility), the Correctional Privatization Commission now oversees about 5,000 inmates.[17]

The facilities contracted and operated by the Commission are required to save the state "at least 7 percent over the public provision of a similar facility."[18] It was the for-profit private prison industry claimed cost savings and the ability to build prisons quickly that attracted the attention of lawmakers. This cost savings claim is very hard to prove or disprove.

In April 1997, Representative Allen Trovillion, the Chairman of the Florida House Committee on Corrections, released a report on prison privatization that recommended to the Speaker of the House not to add additional state private prison beds.[19] Trovillion called on the Speaker to "obtain the services of a independent cost-accounting firm" because of the problems getting true cost savings numbers.[20]

The requested independent cost study never happened.

Trovillion's concerns were an outgrowth of a report on prison privatization by the Office of Program Policy Analysis and Governmental Accountability to a number of questions posed to it by the Senate Criminal Justice Committee.[21]

Trovillion's report outlined the problems in determining cost savings, not only in Florida, but all over the U.S.[22]

Representative Trovillion was also concerned over an attempt by the private prison industry to privatize a complete region of Florida.[23] A report surfaced, which was prepared for the Speaker of the Florida House, reporting on how Florida's prison population more than doubled since 1986 and how there was a "malallocation (sp) of scare resources" by the Department of Corrections, and how the Correctional Privatization Commission's success to date shows a clear potential for private prisons.[24] Therefore, the State should allow the Legislature to "turn over an entire DC region to the CPC."[25]

Ken Kopczynski

This attempt by the for-profit private prison industry to incrementally take over the state's correctional system caught the attention of my employer, the Florida Police Benevolent Association (PBA).

The PBA immediately started lobbying legislators against such a move. We also turned on our "Legislative Connection" phone system for our members.[26] This system allows our members statewide to call the PBA's toll-free phone number and then connect to legislative offices directly without cost to them.

After flooding legislative offices with phone calls and lobbying by the PBA, the legislature decided not to move forward on the industry's attempt to privatize a region of the Department of Corrections.[27] One legislator received so many calls that he sent a memo out to all members and staff of the legislature to clarify his position on privatization.[28]

Six months later the industry floated the idea to allow the for-profits to take over all of the state's prisons.[29] Senator Ron Silver, a Democrat from North Miami Beach, pushed this idea.[30] He told the Secretary of the Department of Corrections to "take a look at the whole Department of Corrections and see if there was any rationale for privatization" of existing prisons.[31]

The Department made it clear it was not interested in privatizing itself out of business.[32] The Florida Corrections Commission, an Executive branch commission, also supported the Department's position not to privatize and the matter eventually went away.[33]

Some think that prison privatization is a Republican mantra. What has been true here in Florida is the reverse. It was under a Democratic Governor and legislature that the for-profit private prison industry developed in Florida.[34]

It was Republican Governor Jeb Bush who actually put the hold on the privatization of corrections. In his second budget proposal, Governor Bush recommended the transfer of the Correctional Privatization Commission to the Department of Corrections.[35] His proposal was to reduce redundancy by eliminating a separate agency for overseeing the private prisons outside the Department of Corrections. The industry was successful in killing this proposal.

The Governor went even further in a letter to the PBA. Bush wrote he was "committed to ensure that current Correctional Officers and Correctional Probation Officers' functions are not privatized."[36]

As of this writing, the PBA has been successful in stopping the further privatization of state prisons.

Into the Black Hole

Shortly after filing the ethics complaint against Dr. Thomas in June 1997 and the resulting press coverage, I was contacted by Stephen Nathan, a prison privatization researcher with the Prison Reform Trust from London, England. Stephen sent me a fax that he had seen copies of correspondences and press clippings about my investigation into Dr. Thomas.[1] The Trust had been trying, to no avail, to get information on Dr. Thomas' funding sources for a number of years.

Mr. Nathan was interested in including the Thomas complaint in the August issue of the *Prison Privatisation Report International*, published by the Trust. He also inquired about getting copies of the report of my investigation on Thomas.[2]

I called Stephen and told him what I knew and that I would be happy to help out any way I could. He told me how Thomas was a consultant for the industry and traveled the world advocating the benefits of prison privatization. Mr. Nathan had always thought there was some connection between Thomas and the for-profit private prison industry but had no hard data to back up that belief.

At this time, I started researching prison privatization and tried to stay on top of what was going on. I started attending the Correctional Privatization Commission (CPC) meetings even though I was the "skunk at the wedding."

The Commission was put between the rock and the hard place because of Dr. Thomas. The media spotlight had been focused on the CPC and while wanting to appear aboveboard, they needed Dr. Thomas.[3] The Commission's August 1997 meeting epitomized its conundrum.

The ethics complaint against Thomas was discussed and his relationship with the CPC.[4] Mark Hodges explained how the Commission had been in contact with the Ethics Commission and how he thought it would hopefully have a decision one way or the other in a couple of weeks.[5]

CCA and Wackenhut were allowed to comment on Thomas after the Commissioners argued back and forth about keeping Thomas as a CPC consultant.[6] Matt Bryan, the lobbyist for CCA, related how Thomas' role for the industry was to "promote the concept of privatization and (Thomas) was going to stay out of all the inter-vendor squabbles."[7] Here was an industry representative, on public record, testifying how Thomas was used by the industry to promote privatization — so much for Thomas' unbiased researcher façade.

Mr. Bryan continued how Thomas was responsible for prison privatization in Florida and that the Commission should not leave Thomas hanging out to dry.[8]

Wackenhut took a different position. Its lobbyist, Damon Smith, testified how Thomas "had crossed the line":[9]

> And I'm concerned because CCA is paying the man and for him to be in a policymaking or even a policy advising process while he's receiving income from the other competitor is a clear conflict of interest.[10]

The Commission was so desperate to have Thomas help write its administrative rules that it ignored all the problems with Thomas and rehired him.[11]

After our June 1997 press release announcing our ethics complaint, Charlie Thomas was inundated with phone calls from the media.[12] Thomas complained in an email to John Lombardi, President of the University of Florida, about how the University was handling the situation:

> Each and every caller requested me to respond to less than flattering comments attributed to you that were said to be contained in an e-mail communication from you to Chancellor Reed... Much as I hate to behave like a baby when hard-ball politics are being played, I owe you the candor of telling you I am offended by the comments you made. I REALLY wish you, or at least one of the University attorneys, had done me the rather ordinary professional courtesy of asking if I had

behaved inappropriately or unethically before delivering the bullet that is now being fired at the back of my (fortunately hard) head by the FBPA (sic).[13]

Lombardi responded by writing that while the University did not see any conflict for Thomas with the school, "there may well be an appearance of conflict with other entities with which you have relationships."[14]

The President of the University of Florida was then bombarded by a letter writing campaign supporting Dr. Thomas.

Correctional Service Corporation's CEO wrote "The growth of our industry owes a great deal to the research and information provided by Dr. Thomas...operating companies, architects, finance groups, community groups', the media, elected officials and government agencies world wide, have come to rely on Dr. Thomas' research."[15]

Avalon Community Services' CEO wrote, "Dr. Thomas is a resource utilized by investors, investment bankers, analysts, bankers, brokers...Without Dr. Thomas and his work, the Corrections industry would certainly not exist as we know it today."[16]

CCA's Prison Realty Trust's CEO wrote, "You have chosen a faculty member and I have chosen a board member because of hard, tangible evidence of his superior credentials, reputation and talent. Now he is being attacked by accusations that are entirely unsupported by meaningful evidence."[17]

To top it off, Prison Realty's CEO expounded on how great their business was doing: "The value of our common stock increased by more than 50% before the week came to an end..."[18]

Mark Hodges also came to Thomas' defense. He wrote, "Thomas never behaved in an unethical or unprofessional manner...(and) several of our top staff positions have been filled with graduates from the University of Florida."[19]

Wackenhut had a different view on Dr. Thomas.

Wackenhut's CEO wrote they believed Thomas had a "serious conflict of interest."[20] Wackenhut included a copy of a *Wall Street Journal* article questioning Thomas' new position on CCA's Real Estate Investment Trust.[21] He continued, "It is in a deep sense of regret that I must ask you to carefully consider Professor Thomas' continued role as Director of the University's Private Corrections Project."[22]

Because of the pressure brought to bear on the University of Florida and the appearance of conflicts of interest between Thomas and the for-profit private prison industry, Thomas was forced to submit to a "monitoring plan" for his University activities.[23] Provisions of the plan included: Thomas was not to use University facilities and resources unless approved by the Director of the Center for Studies in Criminology and Law, where the Private Corrections Project resided; twice a year his activities with the CCA Prison Realty Trust would be evaluated; and Thomas would not disclose or selectively release information gathered because of his position that was not available to the general public.[24]

This did not end the controversy between Thomas and the University — more on this later.

In September 1997, the World Resource Group held its *2nd Annual Privatizing Correctional Facilities* conference in New York City.[25] The purpose of the meeting was to "create a learning environment" to "provide information of long-term benefit" to groups pushing privatization.[26] This conference featured seminars from "Explaining The Growing Appeal of Correctional Privatization," to "Structuring Successful Privatization Projects," to "Evaluating the Performance of Privatization."[27]

The workshop leaders were: Michael Harling, Municipal Capital Markets, a corporation specializing in tax-exempt lease and lease purchase transactions; Charles R. Jones, Wackenhut Corrections Corporation; and Lori Stephens, Stephens Inc, another financing corporation.[28] Dr. Thomas and Mark Hodges were presenters at the conference.[29]

Unknown to Thomas and Hodges, one of the PBA's consultants, Jim Spearing, was in attendance at the conference. He monitored the event, taking notes of what was said. Spearing thought that Hodges' remarks went beyond the "dispassionate observer of the prison privatization process."[30]

Spearing was concerned about Hodges inviting vendors to "come to Florida to help him lobby the Legislature to approve privatization" and to help him in "shaping contract qualifications through the legislative committee process."[31]

What really caught Jim's attention was Thomas' public reference to "deals I've done with Mark (Hodges) in several states (specifically Rhode Island)."[32] This statement would come back to haunt Hodges.

Hodges' bio in the conference packet listed his work for the State of Florida and that: "Hodges is a Criminal Justice Consultant. Mr. Hodges has worked with several states and municipalities including Arkansas, Pennsylvania, Texas, Washington, D.C., and Nova Scotia, Canada."[33] I wondered what he was doing as a criminal justice consultant outside his state job.

In January 1998, associates of Dr. Thomas at the University of Florida released a report comparing recidivism rates between releasees from private and public prisons in Florida.[34] This comparison was supported by a $15,000 grant from the Correctional Privatization Commission.[35] Not surprisingly, the report showed that releasees from private prisons had a lower rate of recidivism than public prisons.[36]

Immediately the report came under fire by the PBA and the Department of Corrections.[37] The PBA pointed out how the report was prepared by Thomas' associates at the Private Corrections Project which received industry funding and needed to be viewed in that light.[38]

The Department questioned the study's methodology, how the private prisons got the better inmates and how the state facilities received less funding for rehabilitation programs:

> "Big deal," Assistant Corrections Secretary Wilson Bell says. "You've taken the inmates who were inclined to be the best, you've given them programs, and they go out and succeed....So do we when we have fully funded programs"[39]

Mark Hodges and the CPC were very careful not to have Dr. Thomas's fingerprints on the recidivism report.[40] But when the report was published the following year in the highly respected journal *Crime & Delinquency*, it had one additional author: Charles W. Thomas.[41]

In April 1998, Dr. Thomas resigned his position with the Correctional Privatization Commission.[42]

At the end of April, I received notice that on May 28, 1998 the Florida Commission on Ethics would hold a probable cause hearing on my complaint against Dr. Thomas.[43] This hearing was to "evaluate the results of the preliminary investigation" by the Commission's advocate, an attorney with the Attorney General's Office.[44]

On the drive over to the Commission meeting, I told Hal Johnson, the PBA's General Counsel, "At least we put a shot across the bow of the industry," because I figured our complaint wasn't going to result in any action against Thomas.

We were about to find out we had hit Thomas dead center and his ship was taking on water fast.

The eight-page recommendation from the advocate, based on a twelve page Report of Investigation concluded:

> 1. There is probable cause to believe that the Respondent (Thomas) violated Section 112.313(7)(a), Florida Statutes, by having contractual relationships with private corrections companies, or companies related to the private corrections industry, which conflict with his duty to objectively evaluate the corrections industry through his research with the University.
>
> 2. There is probable cause to believe that the Respondent violated Section 112.313(7)(a), Florida Statutes, by having contractual relationships with companies that are regulated by, or doing business with, his agency, the Correctional Privatization Commission, and which impede the full and faithful discharge of his public duties or create a continuing and frequently recurring conflict between his private interests and his duties with the Correctional Privatization Commission.[45]

After the advocate made his presentation to the Ethics Commission, there was a discussion by the Commissioners about how the ruling against Thomas might have a "chilling" effect on University research funding. The advocate explained that there was indeed a potential negative impact on research projects like Thomas' but that wasn't their concern.

Dr. Ron Akers, Chairman of the Criminology Department at the University of Florida was asked later what effect Thomas' troubles would have on the Private Corrections Project. Akers said, "I don't like to see the research leave the University...I don't like to shut it down, which is going to happen."[46]

Thomas added that his case "could have great significance for all State University System employees, who would have to face much stricter conflict of interest and disclosure requirements if he's found in violation of the statute."[47]

The Florida Commission on Ethics voted unanimously to order a finding of probable cause against Thomas.[48] Thomas was not even in attendance for his defense. At this point, the Commission would negotiate with Thomas through a "stipulation, settlement or consent order" to resolve the complaint.[49]

Thomas' response to the finding was defiance. He told a local newspaper the complaint against him was "fairly silly and fairly transparently a kind of political move."[50] He told another newspaper that "I have not engaged in any conduct prejudicial to the interests of anybody, pubic or private...There's not one scintilla of evidence to the contrary," and the finding was a "tempest in a teapot" — defiant talk from someone who the Ethics Commission wasn't finished with.[51]

Thomas' ship, and credibility, was sinking.

Thomas' Fall From Grace

Due to the press exposure over my Ethics Commission success with Dr. Thomas, I started being contacted by criminal justice advocates from around the country and the world. The PBA was being invited to conferences and seminars on prison privatization and I began developing relationships with activists, academics and journalists. People came out of the woodwork with information and questions about the horrors of prison privatization and Dr. Thomas.

While the Florida Commission on Ethics was negotiating with Thomas to settle the finding of probable cause, more evidence against Thomas came to light.

Effective January 1, 1999 CCA's Prison Realty Trust merged with two CCA service companies that managed their facilities.[1] In the process of merging the companies Thomas had "performed, and will continue to perform, certain consulting services in connection with the Merger for a fee of $3.0 million."[2] Thomas, facing sanctions by the Florida Commission on Ethics for his close relationship with the for-profit private prison industry and still professing his innocence, collected three-million dollars for consulting for CCA!

I filed another ethics complaint against Thomas on December 10, 1998.[3] The Florida Commission on Ethics held a probable cause hearing on this complaint on March 12, 1999.[4] Again the Commission found Thomas had violated Florida Statutes:

> "(B)y performing consulting work for a merger that led to the formation of Prison Realty Company, by serving on Prison Realty Company's board of directors, and by owning its stock, which conflicts with his duty to objectively evaluate the corrections industry through his research with the University."[5]

Thomas again was defiant. He was quoted in the local newspaper after the second probable cause finding, "I would not expect this to be over and done with for months and months, if not years...This will drag on until I'm on Social Security and don't give a damn...presupposing I give a damn at this point."[6]

Thomas saw the writing on the wall and decided to cut his loses – though a $3 million consulting fee wasn't too bad of a loss.

On April 13, 1999, Thomas signed a stipulation with the Ethics Commission whereby he: admitted violating Florida Statutes; resigned from the Correctional Privatization Commission; ceased all evaluative research regarding the private prison industry; resigned his position as Director of the Private Corrections Project; and would pay a $2,000 civil penalty.[7]

While I was not happy with the $2,000 fine, I told the Ethics Commission at least Thomas was no longer in a position to promote the industry and I would go along with the settlement. On June 3, 1999 the Ethics Commission met to take final action on Thomas' settlement.[8]

The commission advocate presented his findings about Thomas and then outlined the stipulated settlement. At that point, all hell broke lose.

Ethics Commissioner Scott Clemons, a former state legislator, questioned the "pitifully low" fine and called for rejection of the settlement.[9] "If the purpose of this sanction is to deter similar conduct in the future, then a $2,000 fine on a $3 million gain is not much of a deterrent," Clemons said. "I think they have to increase it significantly in order to have a deterrent quality."[10]

The Ethics Commission then voted unanimously to reject the settlement offer to Thomas.[11] Again, Thomas was not in attendance.

The issue of what effect Thomas' case would have on University research funding came up again. The Board of Regents spokesman told a reporter the Board was not concerned about the ruling. But the advocate for the Commission said he "would suggest that the university would probably want to talk to the (Ethics) Commission about what Thomas' case indicates about the viability of UF's conflict of interest rules."[12]

Thomas said he might not accept a higher fine regardless of what it might mean to the University or other universities.[13] "What the university would like most to see happen is to see the morning mail come in containing a letter of resignation from me," Thomas said. "They have said that they're behind me, and I have found them to be so far behind me that I need a telescope to find them."[14]

I was stunned by the Ethics Commission's rejection of the settlement.

Thomas' bow was pointing down and water was coming over the sides.

One of the numbers of researchers and academics to contact me during this period was Dr. Gilbert Geis, Professor Emeritus, Department of Criminology, Law and Society, University of California, Irvine. Dr. Geis was working on a case study with two associates dealing with conflict of interest issues involving criminal justice research that was eventually published in *Crime & Delinquency*.[15] Thomas was the subject of the case study.[16] Geis, et al, would not have pursued Thomas if his name had not appeared in a recent article on recidivism in Florida prisons published in *Crime & Delinquency*.[17]

Geis, et al, point out how when the recidivism report was first released, Dr. Thomas was not one of the authors.[18] Then, a year later in the published recidivism article Thomas' name appears as a "Professor of Sociology, University of Florida," with no mention of his "other affiliations."[19]

Nor, they continued, did the first two authors reveal they were affiliated with the "Private Corrections Project" which has received "$400,000 from private prison companies, with the largest contributors being CCA and Wackenhut."[20]

Another point by Geis, et al, was the Florida Correctional Privatization Commission sponsored the recidivism report where Thomas was a paid consultant.[21]

They continued with the fact that Thomas was a member of the CCA Prison Realty Trust and owned stock in the private prison industry.[22] It was this information that "piqued our interest and prodded our further inquiries":[23]

But, we believe that there may well have been a conflict of interest that seriously (and unfortunately) detracts from the credibility that a reader can comfortably place in the published recidivism research report or in virtually all of the numerous media statements by Thomas that we have located…Thomas maintains, contrary to this evidence, that he has always been up front about his connections as well as the fact that he owns stock in some private prison corporations (Talev 1997). This situation forms the basis for a precept that we want to advance: failure to come forward and disclose in a timely manner what later might be seen as bias based on financial self-interest inevitably will taint and call into question publications and statements that are not accompanied by such stipulations, however accurate the material and however pure the intent.[24]

Geis, et al, then presented the background for their case against Thomas. I won't detail all the discussions because the complete article is available to anyone who wants to read it. One passage though epitomizes Thomas' lack of disclosure:

Thomas had stated that prior to the start of his employment in 1994 with the Florida Privatization Commission, he purchased shares of stock in private prison companies (Commission on Ethics 1998, p.5). Nonetheless, while appearing as an expert witness on privatization before the Subcommittee on Crime of the House Judiciary Committee, he declared, "I have no personal economic interest that would be advanced or undermined by any decision Congress might make regarding the issue" (Thomas 1995, p.2).[25]

Thomas continued in his Congressional testimony that he was neutral on the issue of privatization of corrections but "this neutrality does not mean that I have no preference."[26]

Geis, et al, conclude "Both research and common sense support the finding by Grover and Hui (1994) that 'people are more likely to lie when faced with a role conflict, especially when the reward for lying is combined with the conflict' (p. 300)."[27]

Thomas was now treading water.

The matter of academic dishonesty became quite an issue at this time. In February 1999, the American Medical Association failed to disclose that the maker of the drug Viagra had paid the authors of a sex study that concluded, "that a large percentage of American men and women experience sexual dysfunction."[28]

Thomas was mentioned in an *Atlantic Monthly* article about corporate underwriting of university research projects.[29] This article pointed out how "More and more, professors not only accept industry grants to perform research but also hold stock or have other financial ties to the companies funding them":[30]

> And last June controversy erupted at the University of Florida following the disclosure that Charles Thomas, a criminologist at the school who advised the state on prison policy, had pocketed $3 million in consulting fees from the private-prison industry, in which he also owned stock. (Thomas's views on private prisons are quoted frequently in The Wall Street Journal and The New York Times, and he has trumpeted the virtues of "full-scale privatization" in testimony before Congress.) I'm really kind of astounded that the state university system would tolerate something like this,' said a member of the state ethics commission.[31]

Thomas' troubles with the University of Florida continued. First, the University refused to move on Thomas' request of approval for outside employment related to his position on Prison Realty Trust.[32] He argued that because all of his work with Prison Realty was complete and that it would no longer exist after January 1, 1999, the request for approval was moot anyway.[33]

Thomas also wrote that the Dean indicated "that part if not all of her reason for taking no action to approve or disapprove the request was her expectation that there might be a formal opinion of the Florida Commission on Ethics that would require a change in the policies of the University and all other state agencies."[34]

Dean Lisa McElwee-White wrote to Thomas on January 14, 1999 that she "signed (his) outside activities reports, but without marking either the approved or disapproved box."[35] Thomas responded:

> As I'm sure you and Barbara Wingo (Deputy General Counsel) fully understand, the action will be used by those who are seeking to skin me alive to their probable advantage...I am obviously engaging in the activity; I'm obviously doing so without the required University approval. Not a big deal. I might have done the same thing when I was in your position. Though I doubt it.[36]

In March 1999 Thomas sent a memo to Ron Akers, Director for the Center for Studies in Criminology and Law, about the proposed settlement with the Ethics Commission.[37] In this memo Thomas relates hows "the terms of this agreement will have the effect of the Private Corrections Project not exiting on or after the first day of the coming academic year and no fraction of my assignment being to do research in the area of correctional privatization."[38]

Thomas was now adrift in rough seas and no one was throwing him a life jacket.

The University started fighting back against Thomas. In May 1999, Thomas was sent a letter questioning whether the University would continue to employ him even though he had tenure.[39] Dean White informed Thomas, "Appropriate departmental and college personnel must continue to discuss the (Ethics) settlement in order to determine if its terms are irreconcilable with your employment by the University."[40] Thomas' obstinacy was coming back to bite him.

Thomas replied to the University that, "I long ago informed Ron Akers that I am 'changing gears' and intend to redirect my research...anyway the availability of funding for privatization research has essentially 'dried up'...That quite obviously gives rise to nothing remotely approaching an 'irreconcilable' difference.'"[41]

When the Commission on Ethics rejected the settlement offer with Thomas on June 3, 1999, Thomas wrote to Dean White, "Under the terms and conditions of the draft settlement agreement, the agreement is now null and void":[42]

> We, in short, are back to square one. There may or may not be an opportunity to devise another settlement agreement. My immediate inclination at this point is to allow whatever may hit the fan to do so and to allow the legal issues to be resolved by the appropriate District Court of Appeals. Indeed, the fact that the University informed me of its intention to impose additional and substantial financial sanctions in the event that the settlement was accepted by the Commission recommends against considering a settlement agreement...For now I guess that means the Private Corrections Project is alive and well and that there will be no modification of the FTE (full-time equivalent) for the 1999-2000 academic year based on anything contained in the now legally meaningless draft settlement agreement.[43]

Thomas was wrong. The University was playing hardball. Dean McElwee-White replied:

> I understand that although you signed your settlement with the State of Florida Commission on Ethics, the Commission rejected the terms of the settlement. Since the settlement was always between you and the Commission, the University of Florida was never a party to the settlement. Therefore, the rejection of the settlement by the Commission does not affect our position on this matter.
>
> As part of your rejected settlement, you stipulated having committed violations of Section 112.313(7)(a), Florida Statutes. Our independent review of this matter supports your statements. Further, in the proposed settlement, you agreed to resign a portion of your position...

Notwithstanding the rejection by the Commission of the agreement, this resolution of the problem is in our view the only appropriate resolution of the conflicts between your University position and your outside activities. Therefore, we will still expect a resignation of this portion of your FTE effective August 13, 1999. If such a resignation is not forthcoming, we will take administrative action as the University deems necessary and appropriate in order to resolve the conflicts.[44]

Thomas again responds with defiance: "It would appear that you folks want to take a pretty tough position on this one. I understand the purpose even though I wish 20 years at UF entitled me to more support."[45] He then writes about letting "the lawyers to do their thing."[46]

Later Thomas wrote:

"At this time I have made no decision regarding whether I will submit an unqualified resignation per your request. The obvious reality is that you and Barbara Wingo have put me on actual notice that administrative action will be taken against me in the event that you do not receive the requested resignation and my acceptance of a reduction in my FTE."[47]

On July 25, 1999, Thomas wrote the University to "accept this letter as constituting a resignation from a .34 FTE fraction of my position and that appropriate administrative steps be taken to reduce my appointment to a .66 FTE level. The effective date for the resignation is August 13, 1999."[48]

Thomas was going down for the third time.

In August 1999, Dr. Thomas signed another joint stipulation with the Ethics Commission.[49] This agreement had the same elements as the first stipulation whereby Thomas admitted violating Florida Statutes but this time Thomas agreed to a $20,000 civil penalty.[50]

I wrote to the Ethics Commission that while the new settlement offer was a record civil penalty and better than the first $2,000 fine, "a $20,000 fine in light of Thomas' $3,000,000 contract (a seven-tenths of one-percent fine) will hardly prove to be an effective deterrent for violations of the state's ethics standards."[51]

Thomas retired under pressure from the University of Florida on October 15, 1999.[52]

On October 21, 1999 the Florida Commission on Ethics voted to accept the new settlement with Dr. Thomas.[53]

Thomas' ship had sunk, his Private Corrections Project folded, and his credibility and that of his "research" was fatally undermined.

Corruption at the Top

Clayton Mark Hodges, Executive Director for the Correctional Privatization Commission (CPC), stood tall with Dr. Thomas during all of his troubles. I had some concerns about Mark from the start but I had nothing to hang my suspicions on.

PBA consultant Jim Spearing, reported how, at a privatization conference in New York City, Dr. Thomas had talked about how he and Hodges had done deals together, and how Hodges did outside "criminal justice consulting."[1]

In June 1999, a former high-ranking official from the Department of Corrections contacted me through the PBA's General Counsel. He wanted to talk about what he knew about Mark Hodges, Dr. Thomas and the CPC. We met for breakfast and he told me how he had information I would be interested in and he would be happy to pass it on to me.

This source said I should look into consulting work Hodges and Thomas did. I was pretty busy with my research on Dr. Thomas but I was intrigued with what he was saying.

I went over to the Department of State to review Hodges' annual disclosure forms. These forms are required by state law for certain employees to disclose gifts and other sources of income outside of their state employment. I found in Hodges' file, a 1998 letter to the Department of State that he "inadvertently neglected to include an honorarium related expense" he received in 1997.[2]

This $1,800 honorarium was for a trip Hodges took to Hawaii paid for by Management & Training Corporation (MTC) a private prison vendor.[3] This trip looked very suspicious to me.

I called Mark and asked him about it. He told me that MTC had contacted him about attending their annual meeting to discuss procurement issues with their board of directors.[4]

Hodges continued that he contacted Dr. Thomas about the meeting and Thomas told him that the Private Corrections Project would pay for the trip.[5] I don't know if Hodges understood the ethical implications of this arrangement. The Private Corrections Project was underwritten by the private prison industry. Therefore, the industry would have been paying for the trip indirectly. It looked like an attempt to skirt the law.

Hodges said as he was checking out of the hotel in Hawaii he was told that MTC had paid for everything.[6]

This explanation didn't wash. How did Hodges get to Hawaii without knowing who paid his airfare? Did he put the money up front and then expect reimbursement? If Thomas said the Private Corrections Project would pay for it, wouldn't the Project have paid for the airfare?

I sent a public record request to Hodges asking: Why did he wait a year to report the honorarium? Did he return the $1,800 to MTC when he realized his error? And what work did he do with Dr. Thomas outside of the CPC?[7] Hodges never responded to my request.

On March 1, 2000, I filed my first ethics complaint against C. Mark Hodges.[8] In the complaint, I wrote Hodges might be in violation of Florida Statutes for: "taking an $1,800 'honorarium' from a contract bidder"; "filing his report for the MTC honorarium 30 days late"; and that "Hodges is using his position with the CPC to underwrite his outside 'criminal justice consulting' work."[9] I was going on gut instinct on this latter issue because I didn't have any direct evidence.

In early May 2000, my source gave me a copy of a recent *Correctional Law Reporter* article about Youngstown, Ohio.[10] This article, written by a special outside counsel for the City, outlined the trouble Youngstown found itself in when CCA lost a federal suit by inmates at its Northeast Ohio Correctional Facility (NOCC).[11] It is worth expounding on Youngstown because it is a case study in what can, and often does, go wrong with the for-profit private prison industry.

After the steel industry closed, Corrections Corporation of America (CCA) opened a private correctional facility in Youngstown. The City agreed to give land to CCA, in exchange CCA built a 2,000-bed medium-security correctional facility. This prison was built on speculation—CCA did not have a contract with any jurisdiction at the time but felt that "if they built it—they would come." The facility was constructed to house out-of-state inmates through contracts with out-of-state jurisdictions. Ohio had no laws or regulations for privately owned and operated correctional facilities. CCA was free to do whatever it wanted.

Three months after opening in May 1997, inmates filed a class action lawsuit against CCA and the District of Columbia. After two inmate-on-inmate murders at NOCC, the City moved as an additional party plaintiff in the class action. The City was concerned that CCA was housing higher than medium-security inmates at NOCC.

On March 31, 1999, Judge Sam Bell ordered all inmates at the facility to be reclassified and that higher than medium-security be sent back to D.C.

On March 17, 1998, Ohio Revised Code Section 9.07 became effective requiring CCA to enter into an agreement with the City.

In April 1999, both litigation and negotiation were reached and temporary agreements between the City and CCA kept CCA in compliance with the new law.

As part of the agreement, CCA would employ a full-time monitor at the facility paid for by CCA.[12] Enter Mark Hodges:

> …Youngstown had no expertise in corrections…Nonetheless, Youngstown quickly marshaled its resources and obtained the necessary expertise to assist it in achieving the first-of-its-kind oversight agreement with a private correctional facility. The team was led by the City's Law Director, Bob Bush, and outside counsel, this author and Dave Barbee. Together, we determined that a corrections "interpreter" was needed to help them understand and speak the language of corrections. To that end, after interviewing a number of candidates, the City engaged Joe Waldron, Chairman of the Criminal Justice Department of Youngstown State University, and Mark Hodges, Executive Director of the Florida Correctional Privatization Commission. They helped the City assess the facility and develop information during the litigation phases. Mark also prepared a monitoring manual to be used by the City Manager.[13]

I called Mark about his activities with Youngstown. He told me that the contract was with the City, and not CCA, to deal with all the troubles they were having. He helped evaluate the situation for the City and made recommendations to fix the problems.

I called Youngstown's Legal Department and spoke with Mr. Robert Bush about Hodges and his contract. I followed up with a letter to Bush requesting a copy of "the monitoring manual produced by Mark Hodges" and "any contract or bill for his services."[14]

On May 31, 2000, I received a fax of Hodges' contract with Youngstown and its monitoring manual.[15] This contract told me very little and did not include any contracts or bills for Hodges' services nor the information on the monitoring manual. The reason I was particularly interested in the monitoring manual was that my source confided he did not believe Mark had the expertise to produce the manual.

I did a side-by-side, section-by-section analysis of the Youngstown monitoring manual with that of Florida's. I went through three highlighters marking provisions that were exactly the same or were changed very little. My analysis showed over 90% of the Youngstown manual was word-for-word, section-by-section, Florida's monitoring manual.

The contract did mention that Mark "shall make himself available to consult with the City and its designees...at reasonable times."[16] How could Hodges be available "at reasonable times" while he was working full-time as the CPC Executive Director?

I sent a second letter to Mr. Bush on June 2nd (and again on the 8th) requesting Hodges' "original contract for services," including the "contract for the monitor's manual," and "all invoices Mr. Hodges submitted to the City."[17]

I also asked about how Hodges came to be hired by the City and "at what phone number and fax number is the City communicating with Mr. Hodges?"[18] I suspected Hodges was using his state office and resources for his private consulting business but I didn't have any documentation.

I got closer to what I was looking for on June 13, 2000.

That day, Youngstown faxed me 24 invoices Hodges had sent it for his services.[19] The invoices showed Mark was faxing his private consulting bills via the CPC fax and listed his state office phone number on the invoices.[20] While this was direct evidence that Hodges was using state resources for personal gain, it didn't amount to much. The State will overlook an occasional use of resources—everybody calls home or the repair shop occasionally on the state's time.

On June 22, 2000, I received a letter from James E. Roberts, the Special Outside Counsel for Youngstown, and the author of the *Correctional Law Reporter* article on CCA previously discussed. Mr. Roberts attempted to deflect criticism of Hodges and how the monitoring manual was just "an incidental part of his performance":[21]

> In addition to helping negotiate the agreement, Mr. Hodges consulted with the City to assist it in litigation the City undertook against CCA with respect to its operation of NOCC. The insight and judgment of Mr. Hodges was invaluable to the City. His preparation of the monitoring manual was an incidental part of his performance. I believe you will find that the monitoring manual is not unlike those used in other jurisdictions in that it tracks a facility's compliance with ACA requirements. This manual also is more specific to Youngstown's concerns and is tailored to monitor CCA's compliance, not only with ACA standards, but with the specific contractual requirements negotiated between the City and CCA.[22]

I responded to Mr. Roberts:

> Thank you for your response…I appreciate your support for Mr. Hodges. The question though is his use of his position as the Executive Director of the Florida Correctional Privatization Commission.
>
> We have evidence that he is using state property while on state time for his own personal gain. Be aware that all of this information is in the possession of the Florida Commission on Ethics.

You write in your June 22 letter that the monitoring manual that Mr. Hodges produced for Youngstown was an incidental part of his performance. I don't think that $7,500 is incidental. (*At this time I did not realize Hodges was paid $15,000 for the manual. KK*)

You also state that the "manual is not unlike those used in other jurisdictions." This is very true because the document that you write is "more specific to Youngstown's concerns and is tailored to monitor CCA's compliance, not only with ACA standards, but with the specific contractual requirements negotiated between the City and CCA" is 90% verbatim from the State of Florida's monitoring manuals! Most of what you are using is based on Florida Administrative Code. If this is tailoring the manual to Youngstown's concerns and specific negotiated requirements between the City and CCA, then it must be in the remaining 10% of the document that does not come, word for word, line for line, from Florida documents...[23]

Around this same time, I put in a public records request to the Department of Management Services (DMS) for copies of phone logs for the CPC.[24] In early July, I received DMS records showing a large number of calls to Youngstown, Ohio from the CPC.[25] I now had hard evidence that Hodges was using state resources, on state time, to run his criminal justice consulting service.

I sent a letter to Joel Freedman, Chairman of the Correctional Privatization Commission, asking him to respond at the next CPC meeting to Hodges' use of his position for his own personal gain.[26]

From another source, I received information Hodges might have done consulting work in Alachua County. I had lived in Gainesville, located in Alachua County, for nine years and know a number of government officials there, who were very happy to help me locate these records.

On July 12, 2000, I received copies of Hodges' contract, bills and other documents from the Alachua County Office of Management and Budgets, and the Clerk of Circuit Courts.[27]

After reviewing these documents I filed a second ethics complaint against Hodges.[28] This complaint alleged: Hodges had not reported "a $25,000 consulting contract" with Alachua County; evidence showed that "Hodges may have used his state office and property in carrying out the terms of this contract"; he "may have and may currently be using his position with the CPC to underwrite his outside 'criminal justice consulting' work"; and "evidence shows that Mr. Hodges used his State phone and fax line…to carry out the provisions of his contract with Youngstown, Ohio."[29]

At the July 15, 2000 CPC meeting, I attempted to raise the issue of Mark Hodges' ethical problems to no avail.[30] Chairman Freedman refused to hear my request for Hodges to resign though I did get my concerns on the record.[31] It wasn't until a little later that I discovered Mr. Freedman had a personal reason for protecting Hodges.

On July 17, 2000, I received a copy of the report Hodges presented to the Alachua County Commission on December 2, 1996 and his invoices.[32] One of the invoices listed activities "performed by the consulting team."[33] I was interested in determining if Dr. Thomas had worked with Hodges on the Alachua County Jail contract, seeing how Thomas lived in Gainesville.

One of the documents I picked up in Gainesville was a study, "Privatization of Alachua County's Correctional Facilities? Issues and Evidence" authored by Ronald T. Jones.[34] Jones was a student of Dr. Thomas and later a CPC employee.

To my surprise neither Thomas nor Jones were on the evaluation team – but Joel Freedman was![35]

A newspaper reported the Chair and Vice Chair of the CPC "stand by their director and don't believe he's done anything wrong. Hodges has always gotten permission before taking on any outside work."[36] This latter issue about permission would come back to haunt Hodges. The article also reported how Hodges, "Hired his boss, Privatization Commission Chairman Joel Freedman, as a subcontractor on the Alachua contract" for $500.[37]

Soon other agencies started weighing in against Hodges and the CPC.

On September 8, 2000, the Chief Inspector General's Office (IGO) released a report of an investigation it had completed at the request of the PBA.[38]

I had filed a complaint with the IGO against Hodges and Jones, a former employee of the CPC, for what we thought were violations of the Florida Statutes covering the CPC.[39] I felt Hodges had violated Florida law because a bidder to the CPC paid for his trip to Hawaii.

I thought Jones violated the law by taking a position with CCA after he left the CPC.[40] Chapter 957, F.S. covering the CPC reads in part:

> "Neither the executive director nor any consultant...may have been an employee or a contract vendor of or a consultant to...a contract vendor of or a bidder, for 2 years prior to employment with the commission...(or) for 2 years following termination of employment with the commission."[41]

I had received information from my source that a former CPC employee, Ronald Thomas Jones, had taken a job with the Ohio Department of Rehabilitation and Corrections and had then moved on to CCA.[42] Jones had also been a student of Dr. Thomas at the University of Florida.[43] Jones did consulting for the CPC after his move to Ohio including a $9,500 contract to "modify the contract monitoring manual used to monitor the Correctional Privatization Commission's private correctional facilities."[44] Was it Jones who re-wrote the Florida monitoring manual for Youngstown?

While the IGO report found that our allegation against Hodges was unsubstantiated, they did find Jones had violated Chapter 957, F.S. The IGO wrote there were other issues needing to be addressed over at the Commission:[45]

> During the course of this investigation, it was noted that the procurement and travel practices of the CPC did not contain sufficient checks and balances to ensure proper accountability. HODGES approved

Private Capitol Punishment

his own travel authorization and vouchers for reimbursement of expenses other than travel...

HODGES' procurement practices, because he allows the potential bidders to review the draft Requests For Proposals may result in no bid protests, but makes the contracts susceptible to collusion among bidders.

The CPC does not currently have dedicated legal support... The legal support is also needed to provide the CPC Executive Director guidance on other issues, such as potential conflicts of interest.

FSS 957 does not have any enforcement mechanism. While the statute lists prohibited activities, such as the post employment restrictions, the statute does not provide for any remedies of situations where the statute is not followed. The Ethics Commission has not been charged with resolving violations.

HODGES performed contract work with the City of Youngstown, Ohio, and utilized materials, such as the contract monitor manual, which was generated as a result of the CPC expending funds. HODGES claimed all the materials were public records... HODGES' actions may have violated the Conflict of Interest Statute.[46]

Instead of taking responsibility for his actions, Hodges attacked the PBA in the press: "Every complaint is coming from the correctional officer labor union, and our job is to privatize the correctional industry."[47] The same article goes on:

"The issue here is you have a state commission that's very close to the private industry," said Ken Kopczynski, the union's legislative aide who filed the complaints.

An earlier complaint, which argued it was inappropriate for the commission to hire a consultant who also owned stock in a company that stood to benefit from privatization efforts, led to a record $20,000 fine.

Ken Kopczynski

Four other ethics complaints filed by the union ranging from improper use of state resources to inappropriate lobbying by current and former commission employees still are pending.[48]

I then filed an ethics complaint against Ronald Thomas Jones alleging he had violated Florida statutes because he had become an employee of CCA within the two-year prohibition and he used CPC resources in his move to Ohio.[49]

At this time an associate of mine, Erik Milman, suggested we look into Hodges' court records. We had heard Hodges had divorced his wife here in Tallahassee so the records would probably be at the Leon County courthouse. You never know what you might find.

In the divorce files were reports about domestic violence and a police incident report on Hodges.[50] According to the police account Hodges' wife called the police to report, "her husband left the house with a handgun and was talking about killing himself."[51]

Things were starting to come into focus. This incident happened on July 27, 1998. It was on July 31, 1998 that Hodges sent in his late disclosure about the MTC trip to Hawaii.[52]

A fax memo in the divorce file indicted Hodges took his wife on the Hawaii trip.[53] The memo also pointed out how Hodges corrected two years' of tax returns because of additional consulting income Hodges did not report to the IRS.[54] His wife and/or her attorney were playing hardball — she had the goods on Hodges and he was trying to cover his trail.

I decided to check on Hodges' divorce records from Texas. It was my understanding he was in his second marriage and had children back in Texas. I contacted the Walker County District Clerk's Office, in Huntsville, Texas. Hodges worked in Huntsville for a number of years.[55] They sent me a copy of the divorce docket showing Hodges also had a temporary restraining order placed on him in Texas.[56]

I filed two more ethics complaints against Hodges based on the new information we uncovered on him.[57] The first one alleged Hodges was giving "consulting contracts to a business partner of his," Ronald Thomas Jones.[58]

I had received a fax from Martin J. Hughes, III, an Ohio attorney who was representing the School Board of Youngstown in a suit against CCA. It was the agreement between the City of Youngstown and Hodges "and someone else named R. Tom Jones."[58] Hodges and Jones were doing business together!

The second complaint included documents showing $45,748 in "Correctional Consulting" that Hodges did not report to the Secretary of State and for taking his wife to Hawaii to the MTC meeting.[60]

I still didn't have the evidence connecting Hodges to Thomas. But that was about to change.

In November 2000, I began making cold calls to out of state numbers listed in the CPC phone records. I would dial the number and ask whoever answered that I was "researching consulting activities of Mark Hodges and Charles Thomas. Did they do any work for you?" I struck gold in Ontario, Canada.[61]

Strike Two

The voice on the other end of the line said, "Partnering and Procurement." I introduced myself and said, "I am doing research on consulting by Mark Hodges and Charles Thomas. Did they do any work for you?"

"Yes, they did some consulting for us back in 1996 or 1997."

I had them. Jim Spearing was right—Hodges and Thomas were business partners. Now it was just a matter of tracking down the documentation.

I was talking with Howard Grant, President of Partnering & Procurement. He explained how Hodges and Thomas were subcontractors on a "Call for Proposal" by the Nova Scotia Department of Justice. Mr. Grant said he would look for the records and get back with me.

On November 17, 2000 I received a facsimile from Mr. Grant:

> We cannot find any contract between ourselves and Mr. Hodges and Dr. Thomas. I do not believe there was any official documentation.
>
> I have looked in our computer records and can tell you how much was paid to each of them for their services. The actual invoices are archived now as the dates covered are early 1996 to early 1997. It would take some time for my staff to retrieve these, but we will forward copies to you once they are recovered.
>
> For Mr. Hodges $11,365.44 Canadian dollars.
>
> For Dr. Thomas $10,334.12 Canadian dollars.[1]

I then contacted the Nova Scotia Department of Justice to get whatever records they had for this Call for Proposal.[2] I received the documents in January 2001.[3]

The proposal listed Hodges and Thomas as subcontractors to be used "part-time as needed."[4] This document also listed the résumé's and references for each of the proposal personnel in appendices but the Department of Justice had not sent the appendices to me. So I sent another public records request to the Department for the missing documents.[5]

Mr. Daugherty, with the Nova Scotia Department of Justice, mailed the missing appendices.[6] Both Hodges' and Thomas' résumés listed more locations to research for possible joint contracts.

In November 2000, my source gave me a copy of an article from *Corrections Today* co-authored by Carl Nink, Assistant Director of Prison Operations for the Arizona Department of Corrections.[7]

This article was on the "Arizona Cost Model" comparing public and private prison costs for an MTC facility in Arizona.[8] Dr. Charles Thomas had done the study.[9] I wondered if Hodges had helped him out?

I faxed a public records request to the Arizona Department of Corrections for all contract information for this project.[10] They sent me copies of the contract documents, bills, and an electronic copy of Thomas' report.[11] The contract ran from April 25, 1997 until its second extension September 30, 1997.[12]

Thomas also attended the MTC board meeting in Hawaii in June 1997 during the time he was under contract to determine whether an MTC facility was saving the State of Arizona money.[13] MTC paid for Thomas' trip to Hawaii.[14]

The *Arizona Republic* reported shortly after the release of the report, "by the highly regarded Dr. Charles W. Thomas," that "Thomas' comprehensive study concludes that the Department of Corrections has achieved meaningful cost savings by the award of the (MTC) contract."[15] You get what you pay for.

I found out later that Mr. Nink, from the Arizona Department of Corrections, had made $16,000 as a consultant for the CPC.[16] Nink later retired from the Department and went to work for MTC.[17]

There was a scam going on. High-ranking correctional officials sold their services to the for-profit private prison industry but they kept an arms-length from being paid directly by the vendors.

What I suspected was that the for-profit private prison vendors would be approached or they would approach a community or agency needing a jail or prison. The vendors would then get their "stable" of experts, like Dr. Thomas, Mark Hodges, Ronald T. Jones, or Carl Nink to testify or be hired as "unbiased" experts on why the community or agency should privatize. Then the "experts" would refer each other for more jobs.

I was perusing Thomas' Arizona report when a footnote caught my eye:

> 4 Such a rationale was expressly set forth, for example, in a recently released request for proposals pertaining to the possible privatization of a detention and training school for juveniles issued by the Department of Children, Youth and Families of the State of Rhode Island.[18]

Was this the deal Hodges and Thomas had done in Rhode Island, which Jim Spearing reported Thomas talked about in New York in 1997?[19] I contacted the Rhode Island Department of Children, Youth and Families.

Tom Bohan, Executive Director for the Rhode Island Department of Children, Youth and Families, confirmed over the phone there was a contract between Thomas and his department for drafting a Request For Proposal to privatize the Rhode Island Youth Training School in 1997. I faxed him a formal request that day for any and all information about this contract.[20]

Bohan faxed me a copy of the contract the next February.[21] The contract was between Thomas and the Department but that Thomas "will retain CLAYTON MARK HODGES of the State of Florida" to assist Thomas.[22] BINGO—another business deal between Hodges and Thomas.

In December, I filed what was to be my last complaint against Hodges and Jones.[23] The complaint against Hodges was based on new evidence that seemed "to indicate that Mr. Hodges may have been giving contracts through his position with the CPC to business associates, may have been using his office for his private criminal justice consulting business and has not been reporting income from his business."[24]

I included the information about: Hodges and Thomas' contracts in Canada and Rhode Island; the possible use of Thomas' Private Corrections Project to hide business deals between the two of them; the Youngstown contracts showing Hodges and Jones working together; and how Hodges hired Jones for two projects for the CPC.[25]

My case against Jones centered on his CPC duties overseeing contract compliance by CCA and how he was now employed by CCA, and that while at the CPC, Jones used state resources for personal gain.[26]

Shortly after my newest complaints were filed, the Florida Corrections Commission (FCC), an Executive Commission that oversees correctional issues for the state, slammed the Correctional Privatization Commission's lack of oversight.[27] The FCC reported how it received "public testimony at their January 2000 meeting from two citizens who expressed a variety of concerns regarding Gadsden Correctional Facility (run by CCA)."[28] The FCC reported:

> The Correctional Privatization Commission has no standard reporting format that is consistent among its five contracted private correctional facilities, although a standardized monitoring tool is utilized. Whereas all contracted private correctional facilities have been in operation ranging from three to five years and their respective missions have not been revised, the monthly monitoring reports appear to be an evolving mechanism as evidenced by some facilities only recently beginning to report certain information. At the Commission's June 29, 2000 meeting, Commissioners heard testimony from Correctional Privatization Commission staff acknowledging this finding, and further stating that it does not want information collected and submitted in the monthly reports in a standardized format. Standardized information would be valuable for the Correctional Privatization Commission and other entities as it would lend itself to comparisons among the five contracted private correctional facilities.
>
> At the Commission's June 29, 2000 meeting, Commissioners also heard testimony from Correctional Privatization Commission staff that the distribution of the monthly monitoring reports extends only to

the appropriate private correctional firm's corporate office. Although all inmates in contracted private facilities are state inmates and are assigned to those contracted private facilities by the department, the Department of Corrections does not receive the monthly monitoring reports from the Correctional Privatization Commission.

There are significant gaps in the submission of monthly monitoring reports from the five contracted private correctional facilities. One contracted facility submitted a total of two monthly monitoring reports in FY 1999-2000, and there were four and five month gaps in the submission of reports from two other contracted facilities. The Correctional Privatization Commission does not appear to have adequate mechanisms in place to ensure the timely submission of monthly monitoring reports.

There are numerous errors and/or discrepancies in the monthly monitoring reports as well as errors and/or discrepancies in the data carried forward and reported from one monthly report to the next. The Correctional Privatization Commission does not appear to provide adequate review and oversight of monthly monitoring reports submitted by its on-site monitors.

The Correctional Privatization Commission elected to redirect funds in FY 2000-2001 that were previously utilized to hire consultants to conduct annual monitoring. These funds were redirected to contract with legal consultants to assist in property tax litigation.

In FY 1999-2000, the Correctional Privatization Commission reported no payment deductions to three private correctional facilities for vacant positions that exceeded the contractually allowed timeframes, although the monthly monitoring reports for each facility identified vacancies that exceeded the contractually allowed timeframes.

Florida is the only state that has established a separate government entity outside the state correctional agency for the expressed purpose of entering into contracts for the design, finance, construction and operation of private correctional facilities — thus creating two separate correctional systems.[29]

The Commission then recommended:

> The Florida Correctional Privatization Commission, created in Chapter 957, Florida Statutes, should be abolished and its functions should be transferred to the Florida Department of Corrections utilizing a Type Two Transfer as set forth in Section 20.06, Florida Statutes.[30]

The *St. Petersburg Times* reported, "abolishing the Correctional Privatization Commission…would save taxpayers about $1-million."[31] This cost savings paralleled a recommendation of a Department of Management Services review of state boards and commissions the year before.[32] DMS also recommended moving the CPC to another state agency.[33]

In 2000, Governor Bush recommended abolishing the CPC in his "2000-2001 FY Budget Recommendation" though the industry successfully stopped any effort in the legislature to do so.[34]

More consulting contracts surfaced when I followed up on some references in the Nova Scotia documents.[35]

Hodges' listed as a personal reference, an $8,800 contract he did for the City of Dallas, Texas.[36] I faxed a request to Dallas for the contract documents for this project.[37] I received the documents in early March, which were for "reviewing the City of Dallas request for competitive sealed bids for a municipal jail, etc."[38] A new partner was listed with Hodges: Yvette M. DeLancey-Parker.

My source told me that he thought DeLancey-Parker had done some work for the CPC. I went to the Department of Management Services Personnel Department and asked them to see if they had an employee named Yvette DeLancey-Parker. They did an inquiry of their personnel database and found her records.[39]

DeLancey-Parker had been hired on October 22, 1993, less than a month after Hodges was hired, and she left the employ of the State on February 14, 1997.[40] Yvette Parker had also been a contender for the CPC executive director position.[41]

On March 19, 2001, I made a public records request to the CPC for "copies of any and all documentation you have on Yvette M. Delancey-Parker."[42] One month later I received the documents.[43] Travel invoices beginning in August 1994 and running through June 1996 listed DeLancey-Parker as a "CPC Consultant."[44] She was working on different requests for proposals, meeting with Hodges and the Commission, monitoring facilities and reporting on them, etc.[45] Hodges' hiring CPC employees and consultants for outside work began very early in his tenure.

On June 13, 2001, the Florida Commission on Ethics found probable cause against Ronald Thomas Jones for "using State property and resources for personal use" while at the CPC.[46] While the Ethics Commission ruled against Jones, they took no further action against him because of the "<u>de minimis</u> nature of the violation."[47] In other words, they didn't amount to much.

Another scathing governmental report on the CPC came out in July 2001.[48] The Auditor General found that "the Commission had not established the management controls necessary to ensure the safeguarding of its resources and compliance with applicable legal requirements or had not established adequate record systems to demonstrate compliance with such requirements":[49]

> The Commission's noncompliance with State law in performing custodial duties of tangible personal property resulted in inaccurate property records and exposed the Commission property to possible loss or misuse.
>
> The Commission assigned computer equipment to employees at both their State offices and their personal residences. However, Commission records did not demonstrate the authorized public purpose served in providing employees State-owned equipment at personal residences.

The Commission did not review telephone invoices to ensure that charges were for calls related to authorized public purposes. Our audit tests disclosed numerous telephone calls that did not serve an apparent authorized public purpose.

The Commission has not adopted written policies and procedures requiring the disclosure of all personal, business, Florida Department of Corrections, or Florida Department of Juvenile Justice associations or relationships that could potentially result in an actual or perceived conflict of interest.[50]

The audit documented: the Commission could not account for more than $44,000 in equipment, including a computer lost by the CPC Chairman in Toronto, Canada; numerous calls were either personal or questionable; and the Commission paid higher fees to pay for private attorneys instead of using in-house attorneys.[51]

Hodges responded, "the Commission is authorized to save taxpayer dollars, which allows the Commission to organize in a manner unlike typical State bureaucracies."[52]

Now other people and agencies were taking an interest in what I had been saying for the past three years: the CPC was out of control.

The Department of Management Services (DMS) Inspector General, responded to the Auditor General's report, "Considering the seriousness of the first finding regarding the proper execution of custodial duties, Secretary Henderson has asked me to initiate a formal investigation of the issues noted in this finding, including the location/disposition of all CPC property."[53]

The DMS Inspector General's report was released on September 7, 2001.[54] The investigation revealed the tension that had developed between the CPC and DMS. Lionel Thompson, Property Administrator for DMS, reported:

(H)is personnel made several attempts to inventory CPC property; however, CPC personnel would not allow the inventory. Mr. Thompson stated property labels were issued for the missing equipment;

however, the labels were not affixed to the equipment. Further, since no inventory was conducted, the make, model, and serial numbers of the missing property were not recorded.[55]

Tracey Hill, a Senior Clerk for DMS, said she was not allowed by CPC personnel to affix property labels on their office equipment:

> Ms. Hill stated when the CPC was located in the Building 4030 she attempted to place DMS property labels on their office equipment. Ms. Hill stated Ms. Christi Schmidt would not allow her to affix the property labels and advised her that the CPC would affix their own property labels. Ms. Hill stated she issued the property labels for the CPC office equipment and provided the labels to the CPC personnel. Ms. Hill stated she requested CPC personnel affix the property labels and record the make, model and serial numbers of the property for her records. Ms. Hill stated she was never provided with the requested information.[56]

While the missing equipment was eventually accounted for, the investigation substantiated "violations of Title XVII, Chapter 273, Section 273.02 (Record of Inventory of Certain Property); Section 273.03 (Property Supervision and Control) and Section 273.055 (Disposition of State-Owned Tangible Personal Property), of Florida Statutes."[57]

I contacted DMS to see if it still had the CPC computers, which it did. I wanted to see if I could find evidence of Hodges and/or his staff using the computers for outside consulting.

I did find evidence of outside consulting—and more.

My assistant, Matt Puckett, and I went to the DMS offices at the end of October to inspect the computers. While I was looking at one computer, Matt was reviewing another. I found a copy of the Rhode Island proposal on the computer but Matt won the prize.

Matt searched the Windows temporary files on Hodges' lap top computer. There were porn links on them—lots of links. I asked Steve Godwin, DMS Records Coordinator, if he could secure the computers, which he did.

Thus began another investigation into Mark Hodges and the CPC.[58]

On January 24, 2002, the Florida Commission on Ethics found probable cause against C. Mark Hodges.[59]

> (T)here is probable cause to believe that the Respondent (Hodges) violated Section 112.313(6), Florida Statutes, and therefore orders a public hearing as to whether the Respondent, as Executive Director of the Correctional Privatization Commission (CPC), violated Section 112.313(6), Florida Statutes, by using State-paid long distance telephone services or other State resources for personal gain in his private consulting business in the manner which was inconsistent with the proper performance of his public duties, and that he improperly sold a State-owned prison monitoring manual for the special benefit of himself and/or another. Additionally, the Commission accepts the Advocate's recommendation and finds that there is probable cause to believe that the Respondent violated Section 112.313(7)(a), Florida Statutes, and therefore orders a public hearing as to whether the Respondent violated Section 112.313(7)(a), Florida Statutes, by having contractual relationships with CPC contractor Dr. Charles Thomas, with CPC employees, and his private clients, while engaging in private consulting work on behalf of his private clients.
>
> The Commission also accepts the Advocate's recommendation and finds probable cause to believe that the Respondent violated Section 112.3145(3), Florida Statutes, and therefore orders a public hearing as to whether the Respondent violated Section 112.3145(3), Florida Statutes, by failing to disclose sources of income related to his private consulting work for calendar years 1996 and 1997.

Concerning the allegation that the Respondent failed to timely file his CE Form 10 for calendar year 1997 disclosing honorarium-event related expenses associated with a trip to Hawaii for himself and his wife provided by an entity that sought to do business with the CPC, as well as the required donor's statement, the Commission accepts the recommendation of the Commission's Advocate and finds that there is probable cause to believe that the Respondent violated Section 112.3149(6), Florida Statues. However, because the facts in the Report of Investigation indicate that the report was filed only one month past the filing deadline and that the donor had not provided the Respondent with the required statement, the Commission will take no further action on this alleged violation...[60]

Hodges' attorney and former member of the Ethics Commission, Mark Herron's first comment to the Commission after the advocate presented his case against Hodges was, "I know a probable cause recommendation when I see it."[61]

The only issue that Herron raised with the Commission was the selling of the state's monitor manual to Youngstown, Ohio for $15,000.[62] Herron's position was that because the manual was a "public record" available to anyone, if Youngstown wanted to pay $15,000 for a document they could have received by only asking for it, "so be it."[63]

Hodges reiterated this position to the local Youngstown newspaper when they reported that the "document, unedited would have cost $10.20 — 15 cents a page in copying fees."[64] "It's not illegal to sell a public document," he said. "It's just not illegal."[65]

The Report of Investigation also verified what I had been told by my source long ago — Hodges was not capable of producing a monitor manual.[66]

Hodges testified to the Ethics Commission investigators that Ronald Thomas Jones' only task in Youngtown was "to develop a monitoring manual, for which he was paid $5,000."[67]

The most damning evidence to come out of the Ethics Commission meeting was that Hodges and Joel Freedman had falsified documents.[68]

Questionable Documents

Keith Powell, the lead investigator with the Ethics Commission and someone who I had been working with very closely over the years, had hinted to me that there was going to be more in the probable cause hearing than I expected.

Hodges testified to Powell and another Ethics Commission investigator that he had prior permission for all of his outside consulting work from the Correctional Privatization Commission Chairman Joel Freedman.[1] The Ethics Commission obtained copies of the outside employment approval letters from Hodges to Freedman.[2] Freedman confirmed that he approved Hodges' outside employment prior to Hodges beginning each job. Freedman verified that he had signed the approval letters on the dates on the letters shown to him by the Ethics Commission investigator.[3]

The Report of the Investigation disclosed:

> Additional review of the approvals revealed that all, with the exception of one, dated June 21, 1996 for the consulting work in Alachua County, Florida, were purportedly approved by Mr. Freedman, Chairman of the CPC, on the same day that the letters were written...A careful review of the documents in question also revealed that, once again, with the exception of the June 21, 1996 letter, all listed the CPC's telephone number with an area code of 850. A check with the local telephone company revealed that the 850 area code was not operational until June 23, 1997. Therefore those approvals dated prior to that date were on letterhead that could not have been in existence until the 850 area code became operational...Mr. Hodges had no explanation for the area code discrepancies on his requests. When questioned about the area code problem, he stated, "I don't have an answer for that."[4]

Hodges and Freedman had presented to the Florida Commission on Ethics falsified documents.

In July 2000, I requested the CPC copies of "Any and all documents, regardless of form, authorizing the use of the CPC office for (Hodges') outside consulting services."[5] This was in response to a newspaper article that reported Hodges "has always gotten permission before taking on any outside work."[6] Not surprisingly, the CPC had "no documentation regarding outside consulting services" for Hodges.[7]

After the January 24, 2002, Ethics Commission meeting, I asked Keith Powell what had happened. Keith told me he and Travis Wade, another Ethics investigator working on the Hodges complaint, were looking at the approval letters. There was something about them that just didn't seem right. Wade then noticed the font used on most of the letters was different from the font on the Alachua County letter.[8] That's when he noticed the wrong area code.[9]

When Powell and Wade realized Hodges and Freedman had created fake letters, they set up interviews with both of them to review their previous testimony to the investigators. The meetings were set up in different locations, at the same time, so Hodges and Freedman would not catch on to what was happening or to try to back up each other's story. The investigators were not going to tell Hodges and Freedman that they knew the documents were fakes.

Unfortunately, the meeting with Hodges in Tallahassee fell through because his attorney didn't get Hodges to the interview. Keith Powell phoned Travis Wade, who was to interview Freedman in Sarasota, and told him not to let on about the approval letters.

Wade did a great job of getting Freedman to admit on the record and under oath that he signed the letters at the time of the requests:

> **Travis Wade**: How did you approve Mr. Hodges' consulting work? Did he, did he contact you over the phone prior to his jobs and explain to you what he was gonna do? Um, was it just a letter? Was it…
> **Joel Freedman**: Little of both…
> **Wade**: Okay…

Freedman: It was mainly a, just keeping me informed ah several times there were letters. I don't know if every time there was a letter but eventually, I think, we ended up getting it where there would be letters.

Wade: Okay...

Freedman: Where he would say "I've been asked to work for so and so...is it okay?"

Wade: Okay, um, did any other member of the Commission approve outside employment? Or would he of just contacted you?

Freedman: Yeah, it was just a request of mine to do...I don't think there is any rule about it...

Wade: Okay, so you asked him to, to let you know and keep you informed of that?

Freedman: Yeah, listen I don't think there is any rule about it.

Wade: Were the other Commissioners aware? I mean was it brought up during...

Freedman: Yes...

Wade: ...a Commission meeting or something?

Freedman: Right.

Wade: They were made aware that he was doing outside consulting work?

Freedman: That's correct.

Wade: Was that looked at as a benefit for the Commission? That he did outside work?

Freedman: I can't speak for the other Commissioners but I, my, my feeling was yes.

Wade: Okay.

Freedman: We were very excited about it.

Wade: Okay, um, did anyone approve your involvement with Mr. Hodges on Alachua County?

Freedman: No.

Wade: And you weren't, you weren't the Chairman at that time?...

Freedman: No.

Wade: That's what you said earlier, right? Okay.

Freedman: I don't, I don't think I was.

Wade: That was in '97.

Freedman: Yeah, it may have been real close. I don't think I was Chairman. I'd, I'd have to look and try to figure it out, but...

Wade: Okay, um...

Freedman: I, I can answer this though, I see where you're going with this. It probably wouldn't have mattered if I was or wasn't because this was sort of an informal thing that I'd requested so even if I was Chairman I wouldn't have gone to the Vice-Chairman and say "Would you approve me doing this."

Wade: Okay...

Freedman: Okay, I mean if that's what you want to know.

Wade: Okay, um, now one of the things I was given by Mr. Herron, ah Mark Herron, Mark's...

Freedman: Mark Herron, uh huh.

Wade: Mark Hodges', too many Marks, Mark Hodges' attorney, is the, is these permission slips or I que...I call them awareness slips but...

Freedman: That's a good way to say it though, yeah...

Wade: ...they're approved by you...

Freedman: ...awareness slips.

Wade: Yeah, um, and I, I just need to go over these with you cause, and I guess he just gave them to us the other day.

Freedman: Okay.

Wade: And I just need you to verify that that's your signature? That one's August 30th of 1995.

Freedman: So see I gave you wrong dates, I was Chair in '95.

Wade: Okay.

Freedman: I'll have to look back, I have it on my wall when I was first approved or brought on the Commission. My dates may be wrong on that…

Wade: Okay.

Freedman: …so please don't hold me for that, I'll correct it. Yeah, okay that's…

Wade: And that one was signed on the 30th of August of '95…

Freedman: That's my signature.

Wade: Okay. And is that your signature on the…um, looks like October the 6th of '95?

Freedman: Yep.

Wade: Okay, and this one? Is your signature, ah, looks like your signature on March the 4th of 1996.

Freedman: Yeah, that's the Nova Scotia.

Wade: Okay, I just notice that this one is the same day. This one was signed on March the 4th of 1996 also.

Freedman: Um huh, he was in great demand.

Wade: And this one's another 1996. Did you sign that one? On May the 8th of 1996?

Freedman: Yeah, yeah all of them.

Wade: Okay, and this one is dated June the 21st…it's dated June the 21st but it looks like you signed it on June the 28th, is that correct? Of 1996?

Freedman: Yeah and this was probably faxed, yeah, so that's, yeah so that's my former employment was Bishop and Associates, so that's…

Wade: Okay.

Freedman: …a faxed copy, so obviously I was either out of town or something. This is the Alachua County one, so obviously I was Chair. I okayed him to do it and then later on he contacted me, ah…

Wade: Oh, okay.

Freedman: ...to help him out.

Wade: Okay. So it would have been sometime after June the 28th of '96 that he contacted you to work on that job, okay. And this one, in ah, did you sign this one on July the 12th of 1996?

Freedman: State of Rhode Island, yup.

Wade: And did you sign this one on October the 11th of 1996?

Freedman: Yes.

Wade: And here's the last one. Did you sign this on June the 11th of 1996? Same day.

Freedman: Youngstown, I...I, yeah.

Wade: And I had one question about these. This one is...how are they transmitted to you? And the reason I ask is because you see the June 11th and it's signed in June 11th? And this one is October the 11th and it is signed on October 11th?

Freedman: It probably was faxed.

Wade: Okay, so...

Freedman: Or, or it was sent to me and ah, then I faxed it back to him perhaps?

Wade: Okay. But he would have been the one that typed it up?

Freedman: Ah, yeah.

Wade: Okay. I didn't...there's one, and the one that you looked at I, the one that you were involved with also, the Alachua County. It was different, it looks like a week difference.

Freedman: Yeah, I could have been on vacation then or something like that...

Wade: Okay...

Freedman: ...that may have happened.

Wade: Yeah, it was a summer. Yeah, summer. Ah, okay. And these were um, you know, these were all, each of these other ones were the same day...

Freedman: Uh huh (affirmative).

Wade: …dated the same day they were signed. Okay. That's all…um…

Freedman: We also may have happened where I was up in Tallahassee on Commission business…

Wade: Oh, on these dates?

Freedman: …when they could, could have been some of the times too.

Wade: Okay. Do you go to Tallahassee regularly or…

Freedman: Well, usually we, we, we've cut it down to where we try to have the Commission meeting once a quarter. But if we're into some issues like a procurement or something like that we may have to come up there more often. I've been asked to come up and meet with Senators and other legislators sometimes. Governor's office, that type thing to talk about Commission business. So then I go up there for that.

Wade: Okay. Um, that's actually all the questions that I have for you.…

(Discussion of other issues)

Wade: I was gonna say, that are you a…do they keep these on file? Does the CPC have a, a retention policy for these type of personnel…

Freedman: I would assume that's what Mark did, yes.

Wade: Okay. Um, did you keep copies of these?

Freedman: No.

Wade: Okay…

Freedman: Probably not. I don't keep much of that stuff cause I figure they're doing it up there and, and it's just so much paper…

Wade: Yeah, okay. And for the purpose of the tape, I, this, I mean the letters ah that you signed granting him approval to work on the jobs. Okay, um…that's all the questions I had. Do you have anything that you'd like to add?

Freedman: No, just, just again and I think I've said it often, that you know the purpose of Mark being given, and I don't know if being given permission's the correct word. I don't think anybody can stop anyone else from working a part-time job on their own time. I won't get into those issues that I don't know about but, but at working on their own time, um, but because we, we were in such a sensitive thing I felt it was good to keep me informed and to make sure that he was only working for government agencies and not working for vendors that would end up working with us. Cause Statute 957's pretty clear on that. And, ah, so that's the reason why I instituted this. I don't think Chairman Linder had anything like this when he was chairman. I don't know though, I can't speak for him.

Wade: Okay. It…one, one more question if you don't mind. Is it possible that he may have contacted you by the phone on some of the jobs and, and might not have had a, a letter filed like these? Or did you try to get a letter for each one of the jobs that he did?

Freedman: I think, I think, you know ah, I know at the end of this we were getting letters right away, there may have been a case, I don't know, but I don't think so. I think he was very sensitive to that. He wanted paperwork.

Wade: Okay, okay. Um, that's all I had.

Freedman: And you know there could be…ah, there wouldn't be anyway to tell. When I was at Bishop I had a secretary, but nah, this doesn't look like any of our fonts. Okay, so, I was gonna say could have been that she could have typed one up but no, that's not ours, that's their font. So…

(End of permission letter conversation)[10]

A week later it was Mark Hodges' turn under oath. Keith Powell did the painful unbraiding:

Keith Powell: Now, here's the other question I have for you. When you look at, when you look at these forms, okay? You say they're all prepared ahead of time and submitted to him (Joel Freedman, CPC Chairman). This is, they go back to August the 30th of '95.

Mark Hodges: Okay.

Powell: Okay? Now I want you to look, this is June of '96, okay?

Hodges: Okay.

Powell: And there's a difference in the, in the, ah, the heading on the piece of paper, different kind of heading. But here's the thing I want you to look at. Look at the area code for 1995. Do you see what the area code is there?

Hodges: Uh huh (affirmative).

Powell: What is it?

Hodges: 850.

Powell: All right. Do you know when 850 became the area code?

Hodges: Not a clue.

Powell: All right. Would it surprise you to know that 850 was not the area code until June the 23rd of '97?

Hodges: Okay. I don't, I don't have an answer for that.

Powell: Okay. So, how could this have been prepared then...

Hodges: Right.

Powell: ...ahead of time with the 850 area code if that area code was not even in effect until two-years later?

Hodges: Like I said, I don't know. I don't have an answer for that. I'll ask him (Freedman) and see if he can remember that.

Powell: But you already told us that you prepared these?

Hodges: Right, and I'll ask him (Freedman) if he can remember, you know, cause I don't, I don't know.

Powell: No explanation for that?

Hodges: I don't, I'll go back and look and see if I can, can find one, but I don't have an answer for that one.

Powell: Okay. Cause you can look on this one for '96 here...

Hodges: Right.

Powell: ...and see it does have 904 as the area code.

Hodges: Right. I mean, it, it could be that we where missing one. It could be that I said hey, do you remember doing that, yeah, well let's do another one. I mean it could be that. I don't, but I don't remember. That would be the only one that I could think of. And that's why I'm going to ask him (Freedman). I'm gonna say did we ever do that?

Powell: All right, all right. Well when you ask him then, you got that one, that one, three, four, five, six, seven, seven of them.

Hodges: Okay. I'll ask him (Freedman).

Powell: All right. Anything that was done before June the 23rd of 1997, that, and it has an 850 area code on it...

Hodges: Okay.

Powell: ...that's ah, there was no area code like that at that point.

Hodges: Okay. That's the only thing that would make sense to me, we would, as many times as we moved, you know, it could be there's like, where is it? Do you remember doing it? Okay? But I'll go back, but I'm gonna ask him (Freedman). I mean that's the only thing I can think of, but I'll ask him (Freedman) if he can remember. So...

Powell: So you, so you may have, it may have been some of that, the only explanation that you can think of at this point that it may have been recreated then?

Hodges: It, that's the only thing I CAN think of if the area code is different, but y'all can ask him (Freedman) or I'll ask him (Freedman). I don't know.

Powell: Okay.

Hodges: Well I'm gonna ask him (Freedman) one way or the other...

Powell: I figured you would…

Hodges: (nervous laughter)

Powell: I wasn't going to tell you not to ask him (Freedman) cause I thought you were going to do it anyway.

Hodges: I'm sorry.

Powell: That's all right, all right. Um, Travis can you think of anything else at this point?

(End of area code discussion)[11]

Hodges was coming undone. The Commission had caught him in a lie and Hodges and his attorney knew he was in trouble.

Shortly after Hodges' testimony, Mark Herron, Hodges' attorney had an associate review the possible criminal penalties against Hodges for the creation of false public records.[12]

I thought the same thing and filed a complaint with the State Attorney's Office alleging that Hodges and Freedman might be in violation of a number of criminal laws including: forgery, perjury, obstruction of justice and racketeering.[13] Hodges told a reporter, "It's not creating letters after the fact, it's recreating letters that I had lost."[14]

Hodges again avoided responsibility and blamed us for everything. "These are things that we've already addressed," he said. "The PBA should be doing the job of representing their members rather than doing this to cover up that they haven't represented their members."[15]

The Department of Management Services' Inspector General (IG) released its investigative report on March 14, 2002 into the porn found on Hodges' computer.[16] The report concluded, "Although evidence was found that the laptop, assigned to Mr. Hodges, had been used to access pornographic internet sites, evidence was inconclusive as to who did so."[17] But the IG also reported, "While the evidence is inconclusive as to the identity of the persons who used the computer improperly, Mr. Hodges still bears responsibility for its use."[18]

Ken Kopczynski

On April 11, 2002, under intense pressure, Clayton Mark Hodges resigned his position as the executive director of the Florida Correctional Privatization Commission.[19] Hodges finally took responsibility for his actions, "I've made mistakes but I've owned up to them since day one."[20] The last part of his statement is debatable.

Again, I pointed out how the CPC was not doing its job and how it took the Ethics Commission to set them straight, "I've got to thank the ethics commission…I think their decision proves that the CPC has overlooked Mark's behavior. If they were doing their job and making sure the industry lives up to its promises, I wouldn't have a problem. They are not doing that."[21]

A New Commission

Just prior to Mark Hodges' resignation in April 2002, the Governor appointed four new members to the five-member Correctional Privatization Commission.[1] The new appointments were a response to questions about the effectiveness of the prior Commission.[2]

I had some concerns about the new Commission Chairwoman, Carol Atkinson, former Bay County Commissioner from Panama City. Bay County's jail was the first privatized jail in Florida run by Corrections Corporation of America.[3] She had a long relationship with CCA.

New Commissioner Laura Bedard, the director of undergraduate studies at Florida State University in Tallahassee, also had a relationship with CCA.[4] Dr. Bedard also runs a program, "Women Helping Women," at CCA's Gadsden Correctional Facility.[5]

New Commissioner Gerald Bryan Martinez is a sales representative for Bristol-Myers Squibb in Tampa.[6] Martinez and CCA lobbyist Jeffrey Hartley are fraternity brothers.[7]

New Commissioner Robert Ryals is a real estate broker from Tallahassee.[8]

The only commissioner carried over from the old Commission was Sam Block, an attorney from Vero Beach.[9] Block has been a strong opponent of the PBA's efforts to reign in the Commission and Mark Hodges, and told the media Hodges was "the target of a political campaign to eliminate private prisons."[10]

Hodges' resignation was part of the move to regain some semblance of credibility for the Commission.[11] It was reported that Hodges resigned "amid ongoing ethics complaints and eroding legislative confidence in the Correctional Privatization Commission."[12]

The appointment of a new Commission and Hodges' resignation did not end his troubles.

I started thinking about Hodges' legal battles and wondered whether he had the CPC pay his legal bills. I called Sue Herring at the CPC and she told me that the Commission did pay for Hodges' legal bills. She gave me a copy of the "Request for Attorney General Approval of Private Attorney Services" filed for, and authorized by Hodges.[13]

This request for services was for "Legal defense in Ethics Complaint(s) allegations filed by the Police Benevolent Association against Executive Director of the Correctional Privatization Commission."[14] I then requested from the CPC any and all documents related to the CPC's payment of Hodges' legal fees.[15] The billing documents proved to be very enlightening.

Not only was Hodges' attorney, Mark Herron, defending Hodges before the Ethics Commission, Herron was looking at suing the PBA and me for tortuous interference and defamation.[16]

In one letter from Herron to Hodges about my requests for information from Youngstown, Ohio, Herron writes that my letters to Youngstown "go beyond merely requesting documents or public records. They cast aspersions on your character and your activities."[17]

Herron was also attending CPC meetings monitoring my activities. Herron's billings included: "Received telephone call from Mark Hodges RE Developments/ attendance at meeting of Corrections Privatization Commission"; "Received telephone call from Mark Hodges RE PBA activities/attendance at Corrections Privatization Commission meeting"; "Attended (in part) meeting of Corrections Privatization Commission RE PBA activities." [18]

These activities by Hodges' attorney went beyond just representing him before the Ethics Commission and raised all kinds of questions.

I researched legal representation for public officials in Florida at the taxpayer's expense. I found a Florida Supreme Court ruling that set a two-prong test on when a public official could have their legal fees paid by the public. In **Thornber v. City of Fort Walton Beach**, the Court ruled, "For public officials to be entitled to representation at public expense, litigation must arise out of or in connection with performance of their official duties and serve a public interest."[19] Hodges' legal troubles and Herron's investigation into my activities did not meet these requirements.

I sent a letter to Carol Atkinson, CPC Chairwoman, on April 5, 2002 calling for her to fire Mark Hodges.[20] Either that or seek reimbursement of state's money paid out to defend Hodges.[21] She and the Commission took no action on my request.

On April 12, 2002, the day after Hodges submitted his letter of resignation, I drafted a letter for David Murrell, PBA Executive Director, to Robert Milligan, Florida Comptroller, on the "Questionable use of state funds."[22] There were six issues I raised about the State's payment of Hodges' legal fees:

> First, the request does not pass the required tests in Thornber v. City of Fort Walton Beach...
>
> Second, the request came **AFTER** the Florida Commission on Ethics found probable cause against Mr. Hodges...The PBA believes this is a violation of F.S. 287.059(2) "No agency shall contract for private attorney services without the prior written approval of the Attorney General..." All of the work paid for by this request happened **BEFORE** the request was submitted..."
>
> Third, the request is for Fiscal Year 2001 – 2002. Over 40 per cent of billings paid were for services **BEFORE** July 2001.
>
> Fourth, the request states "The Commissioners have decided to pay for legal counsel"...the request was authorized orally by ex-CPC Chairman Joel Freeman (sic)...
>
> Fifth, the per hour rate agreed to in the request, $150.00... does not match the Fee Schedule per hour rate of $175.00...
>
> Sixth, 24 per cent of the legal services were for activities outside the scope of the Ethics Commission and the Inspector General investigations...[23]

David Murrell requested the Comptroller's Office to investigate the legitimacy of this "contract and to recover the state funds paid out if the contract is found to be invalid, improper or illegal."[24]

On September 9, 2002, the Comptroller's Office agreed with the PBA and withheld $6,582.62 in final leave payment to Hodges.[25] They withheld the money because; "payment for retroactive attorney services is in question as is possible improper and/or nonexistent approval" for the request.[26]

Hodges and the Florida Commission on Ethics signed a settlement agreement on November 6, 2002:[27]

I. The Respondent (Hodges) violated Section 112.313(6), Florida Statutes, by using State paid long distance telephone services or other State resources for personal gain in his private consulting business in a manner that was inconsistent with his public duties.

II. The Respondent violated Section 112.313(6), Florida Statutes, by improperly selling a State owned prison monitoring manual for the special benefit of himself and/or another.

III. The Respondent violated Section 112.313(7)(a), Florida Statutes, by having a conflicting contractual relationship with Dr. Charles Thomas.

IV. The Respondent violated Section 112.313(7)(a), Florida Statutes, by having conflicting contractual relationships with CPC employees and private consulting clients that created frequently recurring conflicts between Respondent's private interests and his public duties, and impeded Respondent's full and faithful discharge of his public duties.

V. The Respondent violated Section 112.3145(3), Florida Statutes, by failing to disclose sources of income to his private consulting for calendar year 1996.

VI. The Respondent violated Section 112.3145(3), Florida Statutes, by failing to disclose sources of income to his private consulting for calendar year 1997.

VII. The Respondent violated Section 112.3149(6), Florida Statutes, by failing to timely file his annual statement of honorarium expenses, CE Form 10, and/or by failing to attach the required donor's statement to his CE Form 10, for calendar year 1997.[28]

Hodges also agreed to "public censure and reprimand" and a "civil penalty of Ten Thousand dollars."[29]

The Commission on Ethics accepted the settlement at its December 4, 2002 meeting — ending Mark Hodges' ethics troubles but not his lack of ethics.

After leaving Florida, Hodges took a position at "Homeland Security Inc" founded by Doc Crants, former CEO for CCA.[30] Based in Nashville, Tennessee, Homeland offers "security management and training to government and commercial clients."[31]

Mark continued his claims that the ethics complaints were nothing more than "a union smear campaign."[32]

Shortly after Hodges settled with the Ethics Commission, I asked the State Attorney to discontinue any investigation into possible criminal activity by Hodges and Joel Freedman.[33] I felt that after settling with the State for $10,000, resigning his position and moving out of state was enough punishment for Hodges, though I thought Freedman should have been punished.[34]

Epilogue

I've learned a lot about the for-profit private prison industry since 1997—more than I wanted to know. I've also learned a lot about how the industry works.

Private prisons don't save money.[1]

They don't create good paying jobs.[2]

They have high turnover, greater than 50% annually on average compared to 16% in public facilities.[3]

Their employees are underpaid and receive fewer benefits than public correctional officers, hence contributing to the high turnover rates in private facilities.[4]

There are also higher incidents of assaults in for-profit private prisons.[5]

I've learned how important public records laws are. Florida has some of the most open records laws in the United States. These "sunshine" laws allow the public access to what their government is doing—or shouldn't be doing.

Another lesson I've learned is how to use ethics laws. These laws are there to keep public officials honest. Use them.

I've also learned to be tenacious. There were a number of times if I had just accepted what someone had told me or I failed to act on a "hunch," I would not have accomplished what I did.

It also helps to have reliable sources. You learn quickly whom you can trust and who is only "talk."

When opposition develops in a location where the private prison industry is proposing a facility there is a high probability of the industry losing that proposal.

To that end, I have helped form a not-for-profit corporation, the Private Corrections Institute (PCI), to help educate the public and public officials to the problems with for-profit private prisons. Profits from this book go to the PCI. Currently the Institute is housed within the PBA offices.

Ken Kopczynski

PCI provides "ground troops" to local communities needing help in providing the opposing view to the private prison's slick PR image. The for-profit private prison industry takes the path of least resistance—there's always another community down the road looking for the "economic development" and jobs that private prisons promise the community.

The Institute provides a daily electronic private prison news service to academics, journalist, activists and others, including industry officials, interested in the for-profit private prison industry.

PCI maintains a collection of lawsuits and reports on the industry and shares this information with whoever needs it.

The Institute's web site (www.correctionsinstitute.org) is full of useful information on those wanting more information about private prisons for folks who don't accept what the vendors provide.

Notes

THE EVENT HORIZON

[1] Transcript, Florida House Corrections Committee, January 8, 1997.

[2] "About the Private Corrections Project (PCP)," <web.crim.ufl.edu/pcp/html/PROJECT. html>, accessed March 8, 1999. The PCP was established in 1989 with funding from Corrections Corporation of America and Wackenhut Corrections Corporation.

[3] Letter from Pearl Bigfeather, Executive Assistant for Financial Affairs, University of Florida Research Foundation, to Ken Kopczynski, Political Affairs Assistant, Florida PBA, dated May 2, 1997.

[4] Memorandum from Judy Brown, to Ron Stubbs, Budget Director University of Florida Office of Provost and Vice President of Academic Affairs, dated February 27, 1997.

[5] *Ibid.*

[6] *Ibid.*

[7] Letter from Ken Kopczynski, Political Affairs Assistant, Florida PBA, to Dr. Ron Akers, Program Director of Criminology and Law, University of Florida, dated March 18, 1997; Letter from Ken Kopczynski, Political Affairs Assistant, to Mark Hodges, Executive Director, Correctional Privatization Commission, dated March 19, 1997.

[8] Letter from Sheri Austin, University of Florida Office of Provost and Vice President of Academic Affairs, to Ken Kopczynski, Florida PBA, dated March 21, 1997.

[9] *Ibid.*

[10] Letter from Ken Kopczynski, Political Affairs Assistant, Florida PBA, to Mark Hodges, Executive Director, Florida Correctional Privatization Commission, dated April 8, 1997.

[11] *Ibid.*

[12] Letter from C. Mark Hodges, Executive Director, Florida Correctional Privatization Commission, to Ken Kopczynski, Political Affairs Assistant, Florida PBA, dated April 14, 1997.

Ken Kopczynski

[13] Letter from John Washington, Esq., Florida Correctional Privatization Commission, to Ken Kopczynski, Political Affairs Assistant, Florida PBA, dated May 12, 1997.

[14] Letter from Dr. Charles Thomas, University of Florida Center for Studies in Criminology and Law, to John Washington, Esq., Florida Correctional Privatization Commission, dated April 26, 1997.

[15] Memorandum from Dr. Charles Thomas, Principal Investigator, UFRF Project #39000, Center for Studies in Criminology and Law, to Barbara Wingo, Esq., Deputy General Counsel, University of Florida, dated April 26, 1997.

[16] Memorandum from Ken Kopczynski, Florida PBA, to David Murrell and Hal Johnson, Florida PBA, dated May 13, 1997.

[17] *Ibid.*

[18] *Ibid.*

[19] Letter from George Zoley, Wackenhut Corrections Corporation, to Joel Freedman, Chairman, Florida Correctional Privatization Commission, dated June 4, 1997.

[20] *Ibid.*

[21] *Ibid.*

[22] *Ibid.*

[23] *Ibid.*

[24] *Ibid.*

[25] *Ibid.*

[26] *Ibid.*

THE FIRST ETHICS COMPLAINT

[1] Karen L. Tippett and Rick Brooks, "Prison Guru Is Criticized Over New Job," *Wall Street Journal, Florida Journal*, April 30, 1997, p. F1.

[2] *Ibid.*

[3] *Ibid.*

[4] *Ibid.*

[5] Agenda, "Discussion Regarding Dr. Thomas & the Prison Real Estate Trust," Florida Correctional Privatization Commission, May 29, 1997.

[6] Transcript, Florida Correctional Privatization Commission, May 29, 1997.

[7] *Ibid.*

[8] Doug Martin, "2nd Ethics Complaint Targets Professor," *Gainesville Sun*, December 20, 1998, p. B1.

[9] Margaret Talev, "Consultant Scrutinized In Prison Privatization," *Tampa Tribune*, May 30, 1997, p. Metro 6.

[10] *Ibid.*

[11] Letter from Mark Hodges, Executive Director, Correctional Privatization Commission, to Helen Jones, Florida Commission on Ethics, dated June 2, 1997.

[12] *Ibid.*

[13] *Ibid.*

[14] *Ibid.*

[15] *Ibid.*

[16] Florida Commission on Ethics Complaint, filed by Kenenth J. Kopczynski, against Charles W. Thomas, June 30, 1997.

[17] *Ibid.*

[18] Chapter 112.313(7)(a), Florida Statutes.

[19] Chapter 112.311(5), Florida Statutes.

[20] Memorandum from Dr. Charles Thomas, UF Center for Studies in Criminology and Law, to Ken Kopczynski, Florida PBA, dated July 1, 1997.

[21] *Ibid.*

[22] *Ibid.*

[23] Chapter 112.3231(1), Florida Statute, "…all sworn complaints… shall be filed within 5 years of the alleged violation…"

Ken Kopczynski

THE CONVICT LEASE SYSTEM AND THE MURDER OF MARTIN TABERT

[1] The discussions on Tabert and the convict-lease system in Florida come from Samuel D. McCoy, *"The Death—And Life—of Martin Tabert,"* unpublished manuscript, c. 1923. McCoy was a reporter for the *New York World* covering the Tabert case in Tallahassee, Florida; and N. Gordon Carper, *"The Convict-Lease System in Florida, 1866-1923,"* a Doctoral Dissertation, December 1964, Florida State University. Carper relies partially on *"The McCoy Papers,"* at the Florida State Archives.

[2] McCoy, p. 3; Carper, p. 332.

[3] Marlene Womack, "Florida's Notorious Convict Leasing Fostered Abuse," *News-Herald* (Panama City Beach), June 24, 2001.

[4] *Ibid.*

[5] *Ibid.*

[6] Carper, p. 333.

[7] *Ibid.*

[8] Letter from the Putnam Lumber Company, dated February 2, 1922, as reproduced in Carper, p. 334.

[9] *Ibid.* McCoy, p. 1.

[10] McCoy, p. 1; Carper, pp. 334 - 337.

[11] Carper, p. 337.

[12] *Ibid.*

[13] *Ibid.* pp. 338 - 339.

[14] *Ibid.* p. 339.

[15] *Ibid.* pp. 340 - 341.

[16] *Ibid.* pp. 341 - 342.

[17] *Ibid.* p. 343.

[18] *Ibid.*

[19] *Ibid.* p. 344.

[20] *Ibid.* p. 345.

[21] *Ibid.*

[22] *Ibid.* p. 347.

[23] *Ibid.* p. 348.

[24] *Ibid.* pp. 348 - 349.

[25] *Ibid.* p. 349.

[26] *Ibid.*

[27] *Ibid.* p. 354.

[28] *Ibid.*

[29] *Ibid.* pp. 355 - 356.

[30] *Ibid.* p. 357.

[31] *Ibid.*

[32] *Ibid.* pp. 359 - 361

[33] *Ibid.*

[34] *Ibid.* p. 361.

[35] *Ibid.* pp. 361 - 366.

[36] *Ibid.* p. 366.

[37] *Ibid.* pp. 378 - 379.

THE RISE OF PRIVATE PRISONS IN FLORIDA

[1] Charles W. Thomas, Lonn Lanza-Kaduce, Linda S. Calvert Hanson, Kathleen A. Duffy, *The Privatization of American Corrections: An Assessment of its Legal Implication,* June 15, 1988, p. 5.

[2] Chapter 85-340, Laws of Florida; Florida Corrections Commission, *1996 Annual Report,* 5.1.1; Florida House Committee on Governmental Operations, *Privatization,* December 1995, p. 63.

[3] Thomas, et al, *Implication,* p. 6.

[4] Chapter 89-526, Laws of Florida; Florida Corrections Commission, *1996 Annual Report,* 5.1.1.

[5] Chapter 93-406, Laws of Florida; House Committee, *Privatization*, p. 63. For a detailed analysis of the problems and parties involved see the Florida Corrections Commission, *1996 Annual Report*, Appendix 5-2.

[6] Transcript of Matt Bryan, CCA lobbyist, Correctional Privatization Commission, August 7, 1997.

[7] Chapter 957.03(1), Florida Statute, "For administrative purposes, the commission is created within the Department of Management Services."

[8] Joint Legislative Management Committee, *Registered Legislative Lobbyists, 1992-1994 Biennium,* p. 50.

[9] Minutes, Correctional Privatization Commission, October 12, 1993.

[10] Letter from Mark Hodges to Recruitment Coordinator, DMS, dated August 7, 1993, attached resume' and State of Florida Employment Application.

[11] Minutes, Correctional Privatization Commission, November 18, 1993; Florida Corrections Commission, *1996 Annual Report*, Appendix 5-2.

[12] Office of Program Policy Analysis and Government Accountability*, Report of Bay Correctional Facility and Moore Haven Correctional Facility,* Report No. 87-68, April 1998, pp. 1 – 2; Florida Corrections Commission, *1996 Annual Report*, Appendix 5-2.

[13] Mark Silva, "Prison Deal Aids Senators' Firms," *Miami Herald*, February 22, 1995, p. 5B.

[14] *Ibid.*

[15] *Ibid.*

[16] *Ibid.*

[17] Florida Corrections Commission, *1996 Annual Report*, Appendix 5-2.

[18] Chapter 957.07, Florida Statutes.

[19] Letter from Allen Trovillion, Chairman, Committee on Corrections, Florida House of Representatives, to Daniel Webster, Speaker, Florida House of Representatives, dated April 2, 1997.

[20] *Ibid.*

[21] Office of Program Policy Analysis and Governmental Accountability, *Information Brief Comparing Costs of Public and Private Prisons*, March 1997.

[22] Florida House of Representatives, Committee on Corrections, *Preliminary Report on Privatization*, April 2, 1997.

[23] *A Correctional Privatization Strategy*, prepared for Daniel Webster, Speaker of the Florida House of Representatives, dated January 15, 1997. While no one claimed responsibility for producing this document, it was generally accepted the industry produced the plan.

[24] *Ibid.*

[25] *Ibid.* p. 17.

[26] Florida Police Benevolent Association, *Legislative Action Alert*, dated March 4, 1997.

[27] Dana Peck, "Prisoner Perks, Job Losses Doom Privatizing Prisons," *Florida Times-Union* (Jacksonville), April 22, 1997, p. B2; Florida Police Benevolent Association, *Legislative Action Alert*, dated April 22, 1997.

[28] Memorandum from Representative Victor Crist via Jim Johnson, to members and staff of both the Florida House and Senate, dated March 10, 1997.

[29] Margaret Talev, "Private Prisons Plan Reprised," *Tampa Tribune*, September 13, 1997, p. Metro 6.

[30] *Ibid.*

[31] *Ibid.*

[32] *Ibid.*

[33] *Ibid.*

[34] Chapter 93-406, Laws of Florida, became law on June 17, 1993 under Democratic Governor Lawton Chiles. Both chambers of the legislature were under Democratic control in 1993.

[35] Executive Office of the Governor, *FY 2000-2001 Budget Recommendations*; Governor Bush has again proposed abolishing the CPC in his FY 2004-2005 Budget Recommendations.

[36] Letter from Jeb Bush, Governor of the State of Florida, to Ernie George, President of the Florida Police Benevolent Association, dated October 9, 2002.

INTO THE BLACK HOLE

[1] Facsimile from Stephan Nathan, Prison Reform Trust, to Ken Kopczynski, Florida PBA, dated July 8, 1997.

[2] *Ibid.*

[3] "Prison Conflict Professed," *Tampa Tribune*, April 4, 1997, p. Metro 4; Karen Tippett and Rick Brooks, "Prison Guru Is Criticized Over New Job," *Wall Street Journal, Florida Journal*, April 30, 1997, p. F1; Margaret Talev, "Prison Expert's Director Seat Questioned," *Tampa Tribune*, May 1, 1997, p. Metro 6; Margaret Talev, "Consultant Scrutinized In Prison Privatization," *Tampa Tribune*, May 30, 1997, p. Metro 5.

[4] Transcript of Correctional Privatization Commission, August 7, 1997.

[5] *Ibid.*

[6] *Ibid.*

[7] *Ibid.*

[8] *Ibid.* See Matt Bryan discussion in "The Rise of Private Prisons."

[9] Transcript of Correctional Privatization Commission, August 7, 1997.

[10] *Ibid.*

[11] *Ibid.*

[12] Email from Dr. Charles Thomas, to President John Lombardi, University of Florida, dated July 1, 1997.

[13] *Ibid.*

[14] Email from John Lombardi, President, University of Florida, to Charles Thomas, dated July 1, 1997.

[15] Letter from James F. Slattery, CEO, Correctional Service Corporation, to Dr. John V. Lombardi, President, University of Florida, dated July 24, 1997.

[16] Letter from Donald E. Smith, CEO, Avalon Community Services, Inc., to Dr. John V. Lombardi, President, University of Florida, dated August 7, 1997.

[17] Letter from J. Michael Quinlan, Prison Realty Trust, to Dr. John V. Lombardi, President, University of Florida, dated July 25, 1997.

[18] *Ibid.*

[19] Letter from C. Mark Hodges, Executive Director, Correctional Privatization Commission, to Dr. John V. Lombardi, President, University of Florida, dated July 21, 1997.

[20] Letter from Dr. George C. Zoley, CEO, Wackenhut Corrections Corporation, to John V. Lombardi, President, University of Florida, dated July 8, 1997.

[21] *Ibid.* See also Karen Tippett and Rick Brooks, "Prison Guru Is Criticized Over New Job," *Wall Street Journal, Florida Journal*, April 30, 1997, p. F1.

[22] Zoley, to Lombardi, July 8, 1997.

[23] "Monitoring Plan for Potential Conflicts of Interest," between Charles W. Thomas and the University of Florida, September 1997.

[24] *Ibid.*

[25] World Resource Group, *2nd Annual Privatizing Correctional Facilities*, September 15 & 16, 1997, The Grand Hyatt, New York, N.Y.

[26] *Ibid.*

[27] *Ibid.*

[28] *Ibid.*

[29] *Ibid.*

[30] Letter from Jim Spearing, President, J.M.S. Associates, to Representative Stan Bainter, Chairman, Committee on Juvenile Justice, Florida House of Representatives, dated October 15, 1997.

[31] *Ibid.*

[32] *Ibid.*

[33] World Resource Group, *Facilities*, "Structuring Successful Privatization Projects," Section 3, September 1997.

[34] Lonn Lanza-Kaduce and Karen F. Parker, "A Comparative Recidivism Analysis of Releasees From Private and Public Prisons in Florida," Private Corrections Project, University of Florida, December 1997.

[35] *Ibid.*

[36] *Ibid.*

[37] John M. McKinnon, "Private Jails Seen Cutting Recidivism," *Wall Street Journal, Florida Journal*, January 14, 1998, p. F1.

Ken Kopczynski

[38] *Ibid.*

[39] *Ibid.*

[40] *Ibid.*

[41] Lonn Lanza-Kaduce, Karen F. Parker and Charles W. Thomas, "A Comparative Recidivism Analysis of Releasees From Private and Public Prisons in Florida," *Crime & Delinquency*, Vol. 45 No. 1, January 1999, pp. 28 – 47.

[42] Florida Commission on Ethics, "Amended Joint Stipulation of Fact, Law and Recommended Order," August 30, 1999, p. 3.

[43] Letter from Kerrie J. Stillman, Complaint Coordinator, Florida Commission on Ethics, to Ken Kopczynski, dated April 27, 1998.

[44] *Ibid.*

[45] Eric Scott, Advocate for the Florida Commission on Ethics, "Advocate's Recommendation," Complaint No. 97-100, dated April 27, 1998.

[46] Ray Washington, "Professor Accepts Deal in Ethics Case," *Gainesville Sun*, April 20, 1999, p. B1.

[47] *Ibid.* p. B3.

[48] Florida Commission on Ethics, "Order Finding Probable Cause," Complaint No. 97-100, dated June 2, 1998

[49] *Ibid.* See also Commission Rule 34-5-020, F.A.C.

[50] Bradley Keoun, "Panel Questions UF Prof's Motives," *Gainesville Sun*, June 6, 1998, p. B1.

[51] Michelle Pellemans, "Corrections Consultant's Ethics Questioned," *Tampa Tribune*, June 3, 1998, p. Metro 6.

THOMAS' FALL FROM GRACE

[1] "CCA Sells to Sister," *Tampa Tribune*, April 22, 1998; A. Keith Powell, "Report of Investigation," Complaint No. 98-206, Florida Commission on Ethics, January 14, 1999, p. 7.

[2] Prison Realty Corporation, "Amendment 2, Form S-4, Registration Statement Under the Securities Act of 1933," dated October 14, 1998, p. 68; Powell, "Report," January 14, 1999, p. 8.

[3] Florida Commission on Ethics Complaint, filed by Ken Kopczynski, against Charles W. Thomas, December 10, 1998.

[4] Letter from Sheri L. Gerety, Complaint Coordinator, to Ken Kopczynski, dated February 8, 1999.

[5] Florida Commission on Ethics, "Order Finding Probable Cause," Complaint No. 98-206, March 17, 1999.

[6] Brian Geller, "Ethics Questions Plague UF Criminology Expert," *Gainesville Sun*, March 18, 1999, p. B1.

[7] Florida Commission on Ethics, "Amended Joint Stipulation of Fact, Law and Recommended Order," Complaints Nos. 97-100 and 98-206, April 13, 1999.

[8] Letter from Sheri L. Gerety, Complaint Coordinator, Florida Commission on Ethics, to G. "Hal" Johnson, General Counsel, Florida PBA, dated April 16, 1999.

[9] Steve Bousquet, "Ethics Panel Rejects Fine of UF Professor as 'Pitifully Low," *Miami Herald*, June 4, 1999, p. B3.

[10] *Ibid.*

[11] *Ibid.* See also Dara Kam and Ray Washington, "Ethics Panel Rejects Professor's Deal Over Research," *Gainesville Sun*, June 4, 1999, p. 1B.

[12] Kam and Washington, "Research," p. 2B.

[13] *Ibid.*

[14] *Ibid.*

[15] Gilbert Geis, Alan Mobley and David Shichor, "Private Prisons, Criminological Research, and Conflict of Interest: A Case Study," *Crime & Delinquency*, Vol. 45 No. 3, July 1999, pp. 372-388.

[16] *Ibid.* p. 373.

[17] *Ibid.* This is the same article referred to in "Into the Black Hole."

[18] *Ibid.*

[19] *Ibid.* p. 374.

Ken Kopczynski

[20] *Ibid.*

[21] *Ibid.*

[22] *Ibid.* pp. 374-375.

[23] *Ibid.* p. 375.

[24] *Ibid.*

[25] *Ibid.* p. 382.

[26] *Ibid.*

[27] *Ibid.* p. 384.

[28] "Sex Study's Authors Paid by Viagra's Maker," *Tallahassee Democrat*, February 11, 1999, p. 3A.

[29] Eyal Press and Jennifer Washburn, "The Kept University," *Atlantic Monthly*, March 2000, pp. 39-54.

[30] *Ibid.* p. 42.

[31] *Ibid.* p. 45.

[32] Email from Charles Thomas, to Susan Ciccarone, Executive Secretary, College of Liberal Arts and Sciences, University of Florida, dated December 22, 1998.

[33] *Ibid.*

[34] *Ibid.*

[35] Email from Lisa McElwee-White, Associate Dean for Administrative Affairs, University of Florida, to Charles Thomas, dated January 14, 1999.

[36] Email from Charles Thomas, to Lisa McElwee-White, dated January 14, 1999.

[37] Letter from Charles W. Thomas, to Ronald L. Akers, Professor and Director, Center for Studies in Criminology and Law, University of Florida, dated March 31, 1999.

[38] *Ibid.*

[39] Letter from Lisa McElwee-White, Associate Dean for Administrative Affairs, University of Florida, to Charles Thomas, dated May 7, 1999.

[40] *Ibid.*

[41] Email from Charles Thomas, to Susan Ciccarone, Executive Secretary, College of Liberal Arts and Sciences, University of Florida, dated May 14, 1999.

[42] Email from Charles Thomas, to Lisa McElwee-White, Associate Dean for Administrative Affairs, University of Florida, to Charles Thomas, dated June 3, 1999.

[43] *Ibid.*

[44] Letter from Lisa McElwee-White, Dean for Administrative Affairs, University of Florida, to Dr. Charles Thomas, Department of Criminology and Law, University of Florida, dated June 11, 1999.

[45] Email from Charles Thomas, to Lisa McElwee-White, Associate Dean for Administrative Affairs, University of Florida, to Charles Thomas, dated June 14, 1999.

[46] *Ibid.*

[47] Email from Charles Thomas, to Lisa McElwee-White, Associate Dean for Administrative Affairs, University of Florida, to Charles Thomas, dated July 3, 1999.

[48] Letter from Charles W. Thomas, Professor, to Professor Ronald L. Akers, Director, Center for Studies in Criminology and Law, University of Florida, dated July 25, 1999.

[49] Florida Commission on Ethics, "Amended Joint Stipulation of Fact, Law and Recommended Order," Complaints Nos. 97-100 and 98-206, August 30, 1999.

[50] *Ibid.* p..5.

[51] Letter from Ken Kopczynski, Florida PBA, to Sheri L. Gerety, Complaint Coordinator, Florida Commission on Ethics, dated October 13, 1999.

[52] Dara Kam, "UF Prof Must Pay $20,000," *Gainesville Sun*, October 22, 1999, p. 3B; Steve Bousquet, "Ex-Professor Gets Largest Ethics Fine," *Miami Herald*, October 22, 1999.

[53] Florida Commission on Ethics, "Final Order and Public Report," Complaint Nos. 97-100 and 98-206, COE Final Order No. 99-21, dated October 26, 1999.

CORRUPTION AT THE TOP

[1] See discussion on this conference in "Into the Black Hole."

[2] Letter from C. Mark Hodges, Executive Director, Correctional Privatization Commission, to Department of State, dated July 31, 1998.

[3] Form 10, "Annual Disclosure of Gifts From Governmental Entities and Direct Support Organizations and Honorarium Event Related Expenses," dated August 4, 1998.

[4] Mark reiterated this story to the Florida Commission on Ethics, "Report of Investigation," Florida Commission on Ethics, Complaint No. 00-015 (Consolidated), dated November 5, 2001, pp. 1-4; see also David Wasson, "Director's Travel Report Filed Too Late," *Tampa Tribune*, October 4, 2000, p. 1A.

[5] Ethics, "Report," p. 3.

[6] *Ibid.* Hodges' told the Ethics Commission, "at some point prior to his return from Hawaii, he was notified by Dr. Thomas that MTC had paid for his trip."

[7] Letter from Ken Kopczynski, Legislative Assistant, Florida PBA, to Mark Hodges, Executive Director, Correctional Privatization Commission, dated February 11, 2000.

[8] Florida Commission on Ethics Complaint, filed by Kenneth J. Kopczynski, against C. Mark Hodges, dated March 1, 2000.

[9] *Ibid.*

[10] James E. "Ted" Roberts, "City of Youngstown Learns Oversight Lesson the Hard Way," *Correctional Law Reporter*, December/January 2000, pp. 55-56.

[11] *Ibid.*

[12] *Ibid.* p. 55.

[13] *Ibid.* p. 56.

[14] Letter from Ken Kopczynski, Legislative Assistant, Florida PBA, to Mr. Robert Bush, Legal Department, City of Youngstown, dated May 15, 2000.

[15] "Contract Monitoring Consulting Agreement with Youngstown, Ohio," between the City of Youngstown and C. Mark Hodges, undated; City of Youngstown, Ohio, "Monitoring Manual for Northeast Ohio Correctional Facility," undated.

[16] "Contract," Section 4, p. 2.

[17] Letter from Ken Kopczynski, Legislative Assistant, Florida PBA, to Mr. Robert Bush, Legal Department, City of Youngstown, dated June 2, 2000.

[18] *Ibid.*

[19] Invoices, from C. Mark Hodges, to City of Youngstown, Ohio, various dates.

[20] *Ibid.*

[21] Letter from James E. Roberts, Esquire, Roth, Blair, Roberts, Strasfeld & Lodge, to Ken Kopczynski, Florida PBA, dated June 22, 2000.

[22] *Ibid.*

[23] Letter from Ken Kopczynski, Legislative Assistant, Florida PBA, to Mr. James E. Roberts, Esq., Roth, Blair, et al, dated June 26, 2000.

[24] Letter from Ken Kopczynski, Legislative Assistant, Florida PBA, to Ms. Betsy Wonsch, DMS Communications, dated June 1, 2000.

[25] Florida Department of Management Services, Information Technology Program, "Message Detail Report," dated July 1999 through March 2000.

[26] Letter from Ken Kopczynski, Legislative Assistant, to Joel Freedman, Chairman, Correctional Privatization Commission, dated July 6, 2000.

[27] Fax from John Johnson, Office of Management and Budget, Alachua County Board of County Commissioners, to Ken Kopchinski (sic), Police Benevolent Association, re: CM Hodges Agreement, dated July 12, 2000.

[28] Florida Commission on Ethics Complaint, filed by Kenneth J. Kopczynski, against C. Mark Hodges, July 12, 2000.

[29] *Ibid.*

[30] Transcript of Correctional Privatization Commission, July 15, 2000.

[31] *Ibid.*

[32] Special Meeting, Alachua County Board of County Commissioners, "RFP for Privatization of Operation and Management of Jail," December 2, 1996.

[33] Invoice from C. Mark Hodges, to J.K. "Bubby" Irby, Clerk of Court, Alachua County Board of County Commissioners, dated August 23, 1996.

[34] Letter from Ronald T. Jones, to Kate Barnes, Chairwoman, Alachua Board of County Commissioners, dated June 15, 1994.

[35] C. Mark Hodges, "Evaluation Summary Report," Evaluation Team, undated.

[36] Nancy Cook Lauer, "Union Raises Ethics Issue," *Tallahassee Democrat*, July 19, 2000, p. 1A.

[37] *Ibid.* p. 2A

[38] Chief Inspector General's Office, Executive Director of the Governor, Office of Investigations, "Correctional Privatization Commission, Clayton M. Hodges/ Ronald T. Jones," Case Number 2000004030001, September 8, 2000.

[39] *Ibid*, p. 1.

[40] *Ibid*.

[41] Chapter 957.03(2)(e), Florida Statutes.

[42] Letter from Ken Kopczynski, Legislative Assistant, Florida PBA, to Marcia Cooke, Chief Inspector General, Executive Office of the Governor, dated March 1, 2000.

[43] R. Tom Jones, resume, undated.

[44] Invoice from Ronald T. Jones, to C. Mark Hodges, CPC, dated received January 12, 1999.

[45] Office of Investigations, "Clayton M. Hodges/Ronald T. Jones," pp. 1-4.

[46] *Ibid*, p. 3.

[47] David Wasson, "Director's Travel Report Filed Too Late," *Tampa Tribune*, October 4, 2000, p. 6A.

[48] *Ibid*.

[49] Florida Commission on Ethics Complaint, filed by Kenneth J. Kopczynski, against Ronald Thomas Jones, October 2, 2000

[50] In the Circuit Court of the Second Judicial Circuit, in and for Leon County, Florida, "Petition For Injunction for Protection Against Domestic Violence," Case Number DV 98-04156, filed July 28, 1998; Tallahassee Police Department, "Offense Reporting Form," dated July 27, 1998.

[51] Police Department, "Offense Reporting Form," dated July 27, 1998.

[52] Letter from C. Mark Hodges, Executive Director, CPC, to Department of State, dated July 31, 1998.

[53] Fax sheet, "RE: Mark Hodges, Correctional Privatization Commission," dated August 3, 1998.

[54] *Ibid*.

[55] Clayton M. Hodges, State of Florida, "Employment Application," dated August 8, 1993.

[56] Walker County District Court, "Divorce Docket," Case No. 4692, In the Matter of the Marriage of: Clayton Mark Hodges and Michele Rene Hodges, filed October 31, 1992.

[57] Florida Commission on Ethics Complaints, filed by Kenneth J. Kopczynski, against C. Mark Hodges, October 11, 2000.

[58] *Ibid*; Jones had received $7,000 to review bid specifications for the CPC in December 1998 and $9,500 for the previously discussed rewrite of the State's monitor manual.

[59] Fax from Martin J. Hughes, to Ken Kopczynski, dated August 13, 2000; ORD-98-254, An Ordinance, "Authorizing the Board of Control of the City of Youngstown to enter into an agreement with C. Mark Hodges and R. Tom Jones for the purpose of consulting with and contracting to develop a monitoring manual and procedures for contract compliance at the CCA facility known as the Northeast Ohio Correctional Center," signed June 25, 1998.

[60] Ethics Complaint, against C. Mark Hodges, October 11, 2000.

[61] Florida Department of Management Services, Division of Communications, "Message Detail Report," November 1996 Billing Cycle, P. 56, 782; two calls were placed to Canada: one on October 29, 1996 and the other on November 7, 1996.

STRIKE TWO

[1] Fax from Howard Grant, President, Partnering & Procurement Inc., to Ken Kopczynski, Legislative Assistant, Florida PBA, dated November 17, 2000.

[2] Letter from Ken Kopczynski, Legislative Assistant, Florida PBA, to Bob Daugherty, FOIPOP Coordinator, Nova Scotia Department of Justice, dated November 22, 2000.

[3] Letter from Robert P. Daugherty, Freedom of Information and Protection of Privacy Coordinator, Nova Scotia Department of Justice, to Ken Kopczynski, Legislative Assistant, Florida PBA, dated January 5, 2001.

[4] HHW Consultants Inc. in Partnership with Partnering Procurement, "CBS Procurement Services Proposal for the Nova Scotia Department of Justice," dated September 20, 1995.

[5] Letter from Ken Kopczynski, Legislative Assistant, Florida PBA, to Bob Daugherty, FOIPOP Coordinator, Nova Scotia Department of Justice, dated January 12, 2001.

[6] Letter from Robert P. Daugherty, Freedom of Information and Protection of Privacy Coordinator, Nova Scotia Department of Justice, to Ken Kopczynski, Legislative Assistant, Florida PBA, dated January 17, 2001.

[7] Carl E. Nink and Judith M. Kilgus, "Comparing Public and Private Prison Costs," *Corrections Today*, April 2000, pp. 152-155.

[8] *Ibid.*

[9] *Ibid.*

[10] Letter from Ken Kopczynski, Legislative Assistant, Florida PBA, to Camilla Strongin, Media Relations Administration, Arizona Department of Corrections, dated November 30, 2000.

[11] State of Arizona Department of Corrections, "Professional Services Contract," DC Contract No. 6814, between Charles W. Thomas, the Arizona Department of Corrections and Management & Training Corporation, approved February 26, 1997; Dr. Charles W. Thomas, "Comparing Cost and Performance of Public and Private Prison in Arizona," August 1997.

[12] State of Arizona Department of Corrections, "Professional Services Contract," DC Contract No. 6814, between Charles W. Thomas, the Arizona Department of Corrections and Management & Training Corporation, approved February 26, 1997, p. 8; State of Arizona Department of Corrections, "Amendment Number Two," between Charles W. Thomas, the Arizona Department of Corrections and Management & Training Corporation, approved July 9, 1997.

[13] Florida Commission on Ethics, "Report of Investigation," Complaint 00-015 (consolidated), Exhibit A5, dated November 5, 2001.

[14] Tom Blackwell, "Jail Consultants Convicted of Ethics Breaches," *National Post* (Canada), February 10, 2003.

[15] Editorial, "Private Prisons," *Arizona Republic*, October 2, 1997.

[16] Carl E. Nink, "Invoice for Services Rendered," for $7,000, to DMS Finance and Accounting, dated December 29, 1998; Carl E. Nink, "Invoice for Services Rendered," for $9,000, to DMS Finance and Accounting, dated April 23, 1999.

[17] Patti Ryan, "Making Crime Pay," cba.org, The Information Service of the Canadian Bar Association, October 2001, www.cba.org/CBA/National/Cover2001/Oct01.asp, accessed June 20, 2003, p. 6.

[18] Dr. Charles W. Thomas, "Comparing the Operating Costs of Correctional Services for Public and Private Prisons in Arizona," Chapter IV, footnote 4, p. 65.

[19] See discussion of World Resource Group's *2nd Annual Privatizing Correctional Facilities* in "Into the Black Hole."

[20] Fax from Ken Kopczynski, Legislative Assistant, Florida PBA, to Tom Bowen (sic), Executive Director, Rhode Island Department of Children, Youth and Families, dated December 15, 2000.

[21] Fax from Thomas M. Bohan, Esq., Executive Director, Rhode Island Department of Children, Youth and Families, to Ken Kopczynski, Florida PBA, dated February 6, 2001.

[22] State of Rhode Island and Providence Plantations, Department of Children, Youth and Families, "Contract for Services," effective September 15, 1996.

[23] Florida Commission on Ethics Complaint, filed by Kenneth J. Kopczynski, against C. Mark Hodges, December 18, 2001; Florida Commission on Ethics Complaint, filed by Kenneth J. Kopczynski, against Ronald Thomas Jones, December 18, 2001.

[24] Complaint, by Kenneth J. Kopczynski, against C. Mark Hodges, December 18, 2001.

[25] *Ibid.*

[26] Complaint, by Kenneth J. Kopczynski, against Ronald Thomas Jones, December 18, 2001.

[27] Florida Corrections Commission, "2000 Annual Report," January 1, 2001.

[28] *Ibid.* p. 79.

[29] *Ibid.* pp. 91-92.

[30] *Ibid.* p. 93.

[31] Shelby Oppel, "Report Finds Prison Monitor Too Lax," *Saint Petersburg Times*, January 6, 2001.

Ken Kopczynski

[32] Department of Management Services, "Boards and Commissions Review," January 2000. Governor Jeb Bush requested this review.

[33] *Ibid.* p. 2.

[34] Executive Office of the Governor, "FY 2000-2001 Budget Recommendation," Department of Management Services, e-budget, p. 1; the Governor has again recommended abolishing the CPC in his FY 2004-2005 Budget Recommendations.

[35] Daugherty, to Kopczynski, January 17, 2001.

[36] HHW Consultants Inc. in Partnership with Partnering Procurement, "CBS Procurement Services Proposal for the Nova Scotia Department of Justice," Personal References, Mark Hodges, dated September 20, 1995, p. 29.

[37] Letter from Ken Kopczynski, Legislative Assistant, Florida PBA, to Dallas City Secretary, dated February 8, 2001.

[38] Letter from Jiroko F.M. Rosales, Director, Courts and Detention Services, City of Dallas, to Ken Kopczynski, dated March 6, 2001.

[39] Department of Management Services, "OPS Employee Inquiry, Screen Print," dated March 12, 2001.

[40] *Ibid.*

[41] Minutes, Correctional Privatization Commission, September 14, 1993, pp. 1-2.

[42] Letter from Ken Kopczynski, Legislative Assistant, Florida PBA, to C. Mark Hodges, Executive Director, Florida Correctional Privatization Commission, dated March 19, 2001.

[43] Letter from Jeanette L. Wilk, Legislative Affairs Director, Florida CPC, to Ken Kopczynski, Legislative Assistant, Florida PBA, dated April 19, 2001.

[44] State of Florida, "Voucher for Reimbursement of Travel Expenses," for Yvette M. DeLancey-Parker, various dates from August 1994 through June 1996.

[45] *Ibid.*

[46] Florida Commission on Ethics, "Order Finding Probable Cause," Complaint No. 00-293, dated June 13, 2001.

[47] *Ibid.* p 1.

[48] William O. Monroe, CPA, Auditor General, State of Florida, "Florida Correctional Privatization Commission, July 1999 Through March 2001," Report No. 02-010, July 2001.

[49] *Ibid.*

[50] *Ibid.*

[51] *Ibid.*

[52] *Ibid.* p. 4. See also, David Twiddy, "Audit Uncovers Missing Equipment," *Tallahassee Democrat*, July 24, 2001, p. 1B.

[53] Monroe, "Commission," July 2001, p. 20, Exhibit B, letter from James D. Varnado, Inspector General, Department of Management Services, to William O. Monroe, Auditor General, State of Florida, dated July 17, 2000.

[54] Timothy D. Carlisle, Inspector Specialist, Department of Management Services, Office of Inspector General, "Report of Investigation (Closed)," Case II-1-6-2002-23, C/Correctional Privatization Commission/Missing Computers, dated September 7, 2001.

[55] *Ibid.* p. 1.

[56] *Ibid.* p. 2.

[57] *Ibid.* p. 4.

[58] Letter from Ken Kopczynski, Legislative Affairs Assistant, Florida PBA, to Steve Godwin, Records Coordinator, Florida Department of Management Services, dated October 31, 2001.

[59] Florida Commission on Ethics, "Order Finding Probable Cause," Complaint No. 00-015 (Consolidated with Case Nos. 00-075, 00-163, and 00-294), dated January 29, 2002.

[60] *Ibid.* pp. 1-2.

[61] Transcript from Florida Commission on Ethics meeting, January 24, 2002.

[62] *Ibid.*

[63] *Ibid.*

[64] Roger Smith, "Panel Charges Fla. Official with Selling Public Document," *The Vindicator* (Youngstown, Ohio), February 13, 2002.

[65] *Ibid.*

[66] See Youngstown, Ohio discussion in "Corruption at the Top."

Ken Kopczynski

[67] Florida Commission on Ethics, "Report of Investigation," Complaint Number 00-015 (Consolidated), dated November 5, 2001, pp. 8-9.

[68] Transcript from Florida Commission on Ethics meeting, January 24, 2002.

QUESTIONABLE DOCUMENTS

[1] A. Keith Powell and K. Travis Wade, Florida Commission on Ethics, "Report of Investigation," Complaint 00-015 (Consolidated), dated November 5, 2001, p. 4.

[2] *Ibid.*

[3] *Ibid.* p. 5.

[4] *Ibid.*

[5] Letter from Ken Kopczynski, Legislative Assistant, Florida PBA, to Mark Hodges, Executive Director, Correctional Privatization Commission, dated July 19, 2000.

[6] Nancy Cook Lauer, "Union Raises Ethics Issue," *Tallahassee Democrat*, July 19, 2000, p. 2A.

[7] Letter from Jeanette L. Wilk, Director of Legislative Affairs, Correctional Privatization Commission, to Ken Kopczynski, Legislative Assistant, Florida PBA, dated September 1, 2000.

[8] See Appendix B, Florida Commission on Ethics, "Report of Investigation," Complaint 00-015 (Consolidated), dated November 5, 2001.

[9] *Ibid.*

[10] Transcript, Ethics Commission interview of Joel Freedman, October 11, 2001.

[11] Transcript, Ethics Commission interview of Mark Hodges, October 19, 2001.

[12] Invoice, Messer, Caparello & Self, P.A., "Criminal Investigation," dated November 7, 2001; see also Mark Herron's "Statement for Attorney Services and Expense Items," November 2001, re: "recreated documents."

[13] Letter from Ken Kopczynski, Legislative Affairs Assistant, to William Meggs, State Attorney, dated January 29, 2002.

[14] David Twiddy, "Privatization Chief Scrutinized," *Tallahassee Democrat*, January 30, 2002, p. 1B.

[15] *Ibid.* p. 2B.

[16] Steve Rumph, Chief Investigator, Office of the Inspector General, Department of Management Services, "Correctional Privatization Commission," Internal Investigation, Case Number II-1-6-2002-53, dated March 14, 2002.

[17] *Ibid.*

[18] *Ibid.*

[19] Daniel Jackson, "Privatized Prisons Director Resigns Amid Investigation," *News Herald* (Panama City Beach), April 12, 2002, p. 1A.

[20] *Ibid.*

[21] *Ibid.* p. 3A.

A NEW COMMISSION

[1] Lisa Gates, Office of the Governor, "Governor Appoints Five to The Correctional Privatization Commission," press release, dated February 19, 2002.

[2] David Twiddy, "Head of Prison Agency Leaving," *Tallahassee Democrat*, April 13, 2002, p. 2B.

[3] Charles W. Thomas, Lonn Lanza-Kaduce, Linda S. Calvert Hanson, Kathleen A. Duffy, *The Privatization of American Corrections: An Assessment of its Legal Implication,* June 15, 1988, p 5.

[4] Gates, "Commission," February 19, 2002.

[5] Florida Department of Corrections, "Gadsden Correctional Facility," facilities webpage, www.dc.state.fl.us/facilities, accessed November 14, 2002.

[6] Gates, "Commission," February 19, 2002.

[7] "The Campaign for Alpha Tau Omega," Epsilon Sigma Chapter, Florida State University, as of October 1, 2003, www.fsuato.net/images/DonorList.pdf, accessed December 8, 2003.

[8] Gates, "Commission," February 19, 2002.

[9] *Ibid.*

[10] Daniel Jackson, "Privatized Prisons Director Resigns Amid Investigation," *News Herald* (Panama City Beach), April 12, 2002, p. 3A

[11] David Wasson, "Prison Agency Chief Resigns Under Fire," *Tampa Tribune*, April 13, 2002, p. Metro 5.

[12] *Ibid.*

[13] "Request for Attorney General Approval of Private Attorney Services," for the Correctional Privatization Commission, filed February 12, 2002.

[14] *Ibid.*

[15] Letter from Ken Kopczynski, Legislative Assistant, Florida PBA, to Jeanette Wilk, Legislative Liaison, Florida Correctional Privatization Commission, dated April 3, 2002.

[16] Letter from Mark Herron, Akerman Senterfitt, to C. Mark Hodges, Executive Director, Correctional Privatization Commission, RE: PBA letters to Ohio Officials, dated July 5, 2000.

[17] *Ibid.*

[18] Herron, "Invoice for Services," through 30-Nov-00.

[19] **Thornber v. City of Fort Walton Beach**, *Fla. Sup. Ct. October 11, 1990, 568 So. 2d 914.*

[20] Letter from Ken Kopczynski, Legislative Assistant, Florida PBA, to Carol Atkinson, Chair, Correctional Privatization Commission, dated April 5, 2002.

[21] *Ibid.*

[22] Letter from David Murrell, Executive Director, Florida PBA, to Robert Milligan, Florida Comptroller, dated April 12, 2002.

[23] *Ibid.*

[24] *Ibid.*

[25] Tom Wade, Investigator, Florida Comptroller's Office, "Case Closing Request," IV 20020500005, dated May 2, 2002.

[26] *Ibid.*

[27] Florida Commission on Ethics, "Joint Stipulation of Fact, Law, and Recommended Order," signed November 6, 2002.

[28] *Ibid.* p. 2.

[29] *Ibid.* p. 4.

[30] David Wasson, "Ex-Prison Official Admits Violations," *Tampa Tribune*, November 14, 2002, p. 6B.

[31] Getahn Ward, "Crants Pins Comeback On Homeland Security," *Tennessean* (Nashville), May 23, 2002.

[32] Wasson, "Violations," p. 6B.

[33] Letter from Ken Kopczynski, Legislative Affairs Assistant, Florida PBA, to William Meggs, State Attorney, dated December 13, 2002.

[34] *Ibid.*

EPILOGUE

[1] There are a number of independent studies showing there is no real cost savings by privatizing prisons or jails, see: General Accounting Office. 1991. *Private Prisons: Cost Savings and BOP Statutory Authority Need to Be Resolved.* GAO/GDD-91-21, February 7, 1991. Washington, D.C; U.S. General Accounting Office; 8.;GAO. 1996. *Private and Public Prisons: Studies Comparing Operational Cost and/or Quality of Service.* GAO/GDD-96-158. Washington, D.C.: U.S. General Accounting Office: 8.; McDonald, Elizabeth Fournier, Malcolm Russell-Einhorn and Stephen Crawford. 1998. *Private Prisons in the United States: An Assessment of Current Practice.* Cambridge, MA.: Abt Associates, Inc.

[2] Average entry-level salary for public officers in 2000 was $23,002 and maximum officer salary was $36,328 while private's paid $17,628 and $22,082 respectively. Camille Graham Camp and George M. Camp, "The Corrections 2000 Yearbook Private Correctional Facilities," 2000, p. 98; and Camp and Camp, "The Corrections 2000 Yearbook Adult Corrections," 2000, p. 155.

[3] "Private Corrections," p. 22, and "Adult Corrections," p. 152. These numbers reflect Florida's turnover rates.

[4] Scott D. Camp and Gerald G. Gaes, "Growth and Quality of U.S. Private Prisons: Evidence from a National Survey," Federal Bureau of Prison, Office of Research and Evaluation, October 23, 2001, p. 2-3.

[5] James Austin and Garry Coventry, *Emerging Issues on Private Prisons*, Washington, D.C., Bureau of Justice Assistance, 2001.

About the Author

Since 1993, Ken Kopczynski has been a Legislative and Political Affairs Assistant for the Florida Police Benevolent Association, the largest collective bargaining agent for law enforcement, correctional and correctional probation officers in Florida. He lobbies on behalf of officers, conducts research and analysis, and provides campaign consulting. Ken is also the Executive Director for the Private Corrections Institute, established to educate the public about the for-profit private prison industry.

Ken received his Bachelor of Science degree in Political Science from the Florida State University with a minor in Political Communications in 1992. He is married to Dr. Penelope Kirby, an assistant professor of mathematics at Florida State University. They have two children, Tristan and Katriana, a dog, a hamster, and a house full of cats.

Ken is an artist who paints, sculpts and makes jewelry. He also likes to play the piano and guitar whenever he can.

www.ingramcontent.com/pod-product-compliance
Lightning Source LLC
Chambersburg PA
CBHW051438280526
45785CB00003B/1336